CAMBRIDGE LIBRARY COLLECTION

Books of enduring scholarly value

Literary Studies

This series provides a high-quality selection of early printings of literary works, textual editions, anthologies and literary criticism which are of lasting scholarly interest. Ranging from Old English to Shakespeare to early twentieth-century work from around the world, these books offer a valuable resource for scholars in reception history, textual editing, and literary studies.

Life of George Eliot

'George Eliot' was the pseudonym of Marian Evans (1819–80), possibly the greatest of the Victorian novelists, whose works include *The Mill on the Floss* (1860), *Middlemarch* (1871–2) and *Daniel Deronda* (1876). Her personal life was complex – she was an independent woman who challenged social conventions. Her friend, Eton master and historian Oscar Browning (1837–1923), was moved to write this affectionate assessment of her life, and it was published in 1890, offering 'no claims … but a friendship of fifteen years, and a deep and unswerving devotion to her mind and character'. Browning takes a chronological approach, focusing mainly on the beginnings of Eliot's writing career and on her novels, while adding recollections of their encounters. He also writes with candour about Eliot's relationship and cohabitation with the married writer G. H. Lewes (1817–78), which transgressed the social norms of the period.

T0371275

Life of George Eliot

Oscar Browning

CAMBRIDGE
UNIVERSITY PRESS

CAMBRIDGE UNIVERSITY PRESS

Cambridge, New York, Melbourne, Madrid, Cape Town,
Singapore, São Paolo, Delhi, Tokyo, Mexico City

Published in the United States of America by Cambridge University Press, New York

www.cambridge.org
Information on this title: www.cambridge.org/9781108040495

© in this compilation Cambridge University Press 2012

This edition first published 1890
This digitally printed version 2012

ISBN 978-1-108-04049-5 Paperback

"Great Writers."

EDITED BY

PROFESSOR ERIC S. ROBERTSON, M.A.

LIFE OF GEORGE ELIOT.

TO

THE MEMORY

OF

MY MOTHER.

LIFE

OF

GEORGE ELIOT

BY

OSCAR BROWNING

LONDON

WALTER SCOTT, 24, WARWICK LANE

1890

CONTENTS.

CHAPTER I.

CHAPTER II.

CHAPTER III.

CHAPTER IV.

CHAPTER V.

NOTE.

—♦♦—

THIS book could not have been written without constant reference to the "Life and Letters of George Eliot," published by her husband, Mr. John Cross. I have had access to a considerable number of unpublished letters, but I have only thought it desirable to print four of them. Information about the localities described by George Eliot has been drawn partly from Mr. Parkinson's useful book, "George Eliot's Country," and partly from personal knowledge. The last chapter of this work was originally published in the *Fortnightly Review*, nearly in its present form.

LIFE OF GEORGE ELIOT.

—♦—

CHAPTER I

THE name of George Eliot is unique in English literature. No woman has attained so high a place among the writers of our country. But, omitting considerations of sex, it is remarkable that any one with so few apparent advantages, with engagements which were unfavourable to the literary life, with a strong distrust of self within, and little stimulus or assistance from without, should, beginning original production after middle life, have executed so large a quantity of work of the highest merit and of far-reaching influence. At this moment, ten years after her death, it is perhaps most difficult to forecast what will be her ultimate position. Reputations which stand highest at the period of a sudden dissolution, pass for a season into obscurity. No longer regarded as contemporary, they must wait for the verdict of posterity. George Eliot has often been spoken of as a modern Shakspeare. Full of the racy sap of the English Midlands, her novels, although drawn, as all good art must be drawn, from experience, are objective and impersonal in form. There is also a strong analogy between the modern novel and the drama of a past age. In a good novel descriptions are few, conversations many. A character is not analyzed by the author, but suffered to develop itself by speech and action. No English novels have aimed at higher ends, have presented more complex characters, or attempted more difficult problems. What is the essential difference between "Werther" and "Goetz von Berlichingen," between "Faust" and "Wilhelm Meister"? Goethe, a writer of drama, allowed himself more narrative in the novel. It is possible that "Adam Bede," "Middlemarch," and "Daniel Deronda" may eventually have their place rather beside "Hamlet" and "Macbeth" than beside "Tom Jones" and "Clarissa Harlowe." But in the general applause of critics a note of dissatisfaction is audible, which may grow louder as time advances. It is said that the language of George Eliot is forced and pedantic, her characters unreal, her tendency to preach and instruct too evident. The reader is too continually before her mind; she anticipates his judgments, and tells him what he ought to feel. On the other hand, it is possible that she is the creator of a new style, and that coming generations will appreciate and imitate her, as the greatest musicians wrote not for their own half-century, but for the next.

The present volume, in its short compass, aims at being both a biography and a criticism. Such a book has her own approval.

"We have often wished," she says, "that when some great or good personage dies, instead of the dreary three- or five-volumed compilation of letters and diary and detail, little to the purpose, which two-thirds of the reading public have not the chance, nor on the other hand the inclination, to read, we could have a real ' Life,' setting forth briefly and vividly the many inward and outward struggles, aims and achievements, so as to make clear the meaning which his experience has for his fellows."

The present writer is conscious how little he is qualified to fulfil this ideal. He has no claims to offer but a friend-ship of fifteen years, and a deep and unswerving devotion to her mind and character. No attempt will be made to relate new facts in her life. The Life written by her husband must remain for a long time the received and invariable account. To relate new facts imperfectly verified, and uncorrelated with the whole story of the life, might gratify an unhealthy curiosity, but would con-duce to misconception. Some day, perhaps, George Eliot will undergo the fate of Goethe. We shall know how she spent every week of her existence, and how far the scenes of her novels, even the most sensational, are records of her own trials and experiences. But Mr. Cross has attempted very little of literary criticism, and the field is still open for a work which, while respecting his reticence and good taste, aims at describing at once the woman and the author.

Mary Ann Evans was born at South Farm, Arbury, on St. Cecilia's Day, November 22, 1819. Her father was Robert Evans, the son of George Evans, who was a carpenter and a builder in the small hamlet of Roston, which lies on the very edge of Derbyshire, overlooking the Dove and the hills of Staffordshire beyond. The family were originally Welsh, and came from Northop, in Flintshire. Robert Evans, when he was grown up, moved to the lovely village of Ellastone, in Staffordshire, divided only by a bridge from Norbury, of which Roston is almost a part. As a young man Robert Evans became connected with the Newdigate family. He formed with Mr. Francis Newdigate a friendship similar to that between Adam Bede and Arthur Donnithorne. Mr. Newdigate appointed him as his agent at Kirk Hallam, on the other side of the county; but a few years later, on succeeding to the Warwickshire estate, Mr. Newdigate took Robert Evans with him. Three years later his first wife died, leaving him with two children, the second of whom, Frances Lucy, afterwards Mrs. Houghton, had great influence over her younger sister. After four years widowhood George Eliot's father married again, and had three children, of whom Mary Ann was the youngest, being born when her father was forty-eight years old. Her brother Isaac, the Tom Tulliver of "The Mill on the Floss," and the "brother" of the Sonnets, was her senior by three years. The South Farm, Arbury, stands within the limits of Arbury Park, and is approached from the carriage drive through a short avenue of lofty elms. It is described as a small, low-roofed farmhouse, nestling behind a clump of trees, with open flat fields stretching away to the south. It has a neat and well-kept garden, with cosy grounds and surroundings. Within a day's walk of this little farmhouse, as Mr. D. Parkinson tells us,[1] are all the spots and places

---

[1] "Scenes from the 'George Eliot' Country." Leeds, 1888. I am indebted to Mr. Parkinson for many of the local details which are given in these pages.

made interesting from their association with the "Scenes
of Clerical Life." Looking up the avenue of elms and
across the park, one sees, less than a mile distant, the
front of Arbury Hall, the Cheverel Manor of " Mr. Gilfil's
Love-Story." To the west, about a mile distant, topping
a hill, stands Astley Church, the "Knebley Church" of
the story. To the north is Stockingford, the "Padiham
Common" of "Janet's Repentance." Five miles distant,
in the "flat, low-lying fields," is the town of Nuneaton,
the "Milby" of the same story; while a straggling
suburb of it is Chilvers Coton, known in the "Sad
Fortunes of the Rev. Amos Barton" under the name of
"Shepperton."

In March, 1820, when Mary Ann was four months
old, her family removed to Griff House, which stands on
the high road a little more than a mile from Nuneaton.
It is a picturesque old residence, two stories high, more
like a manor house than a farm house. It is built of
deep red brick, covered with ivy. A lawn in front is
planted with tall trees. Behind the house are the farm
buildings, and a large garden with an old summer-house,
rich in memories of the novelist's childhood. The garden
is described in "Adam Bede" as "a true farm-house
garden, with hardy perennial flowers, unpruned fruit-
trees, and kitchen vegetables growing together in careless,
half-neglected abundance." "There were tall hollyhocks
beginning to flower and dazzle the eye with their pink,
white, and yellow; there were the syringas and Gueldres
roses, all large and disorderly for want of trimming;
there were leafy walls of scarlet beans and late peas;
there was a row of bushy filberts in one direction, and in

another a huge apple-tree making a barren circle under
its low-spreading boughs." Round the labourers' cottages,
which are close to Griff House, are refuse heaps from
deserted coal and iron pits, now changed into grass-
grown mounds of earth. At the back of the house are
paths leading to the "Round Pool," the "rookery
elms," and to the Griff Hollows, where, under the name
of the "Red Deeps," Maggie Tulliver used to meet
Philip Wakem.

In this house Mary Ann Evans spent the first twenty-
one years of her life. Here she grew up with her
brother "like two buds that kiss" each other on the
slightest impulse. As he trudged along she lagged behind,
or trotted after him like a puppy. From this house they
wandered together with rod and line towards the far-off
stream.

> " Our mother bade us keep the trodden ways,
>   Stroked down my tippet, set my brother's frill,
>   Then with the benediction of her gaze
>   Clung to us lessening, and pursued us still
>   Across the homestead, to the rookery elms."

The great events of the day were the passing of the coaches
before the gate of Griff House, which lies at the bend
of the road between Coventry and Nuneaton. Two
coaches passed the door daily—one from Birmingham at
ten o'clock in the morning, and the other from Stamford
at three in the afternoon. The children used to watch
for their appearance eagerly from the window. George
Eliot's mother, Christiana Pearson, was a shrewd,
practical woman, not unlike Mrs. Poyser in "Adam

Bede," or Mrs. Hackit in the "Scenes from Clerical Life." She was at the time of her marriage slightly above her husband in social position. Mr. Cross says: "Her family are, no doubt, prototypes of the Dodsons in 'The Mill on the Floss.'" There were three other married sisters living in the neighbourhood of Griff, and probably Mr. Evans heard a good deal about the traditions of the Pearson family.

George Eliot received her first lessons in the cottage of a Mrs. Moore, who kept a dame's school close to the gates of Griff. She was not a precocious child, but learned to read with some difficulty, and was very fond of play. Mr. Cross says of her—"In her moral development she showed, from the earliest years, the trait that was most marked in her through life—namely, the absolute need of some one person who should be all in all to her, and to whom she should be all in all. Very jealous in her affections, and easily moved to smiles or tears, she was of a nature capable of the keenest enjoyment and the keenest suffering, 'knowing all the wealth and all the woe' of a pre-eminently exclusive disposition. She was affectionate, proud, and sensitive in the highest degree."

At the age of five she went to join her sister Christiana at a school kept by a Miss Lathom, at Attleborough, a suburb of Nuneaton. Here the two sisters continued as boarders for three or four years. The schoolhouse and schoolrooms still exist, and are still devoted to the same purpose. It is described by Mr. Parkinson as a sweet little dwelling-house, covered with ivy, with everything about it scrupulously orderly and clean. The memory of

2

Mary Ann Evans still lingers about the place "as an
awkward girl, reserved and serious far beyond her years,
but observant and addicted to the habit of sitting in
corners and watching her elders." Indeed a certain
awkwardness of manner was a salient characteristic of
George Eliot, and did not entirely disappear till the
last ten years of her life, when it was absorbed in
that kindly and majestic grace which has impressed itself on so many who have recorded her appearance. The
sisters came home to Griff every Saturday, but Mary
Ann's great delight was to join her brother once again
in the holidays and to discover all that he had been
doing and learning in her absence. The elder sister
Chrissey was always very neat and tidy, and was the
favourite of the aunts, whereas Mary Ann and her
brother were always together. The boy was her mother's
pet, and the girl her father's. He often took her with
him in his drives about the country. She stood between
his knees as he drove leisurely along, and drank in
everything with observant eyes.

The first book she ever read was " The Linnet's Life,"
a present from her father. An old friend of the family
also gave her books which she read again and again
until she knew them by heart. Among them were Æsop's
Fables and Joe Miller's jest-book. When she was
seven years old she left home for the first time for a
week's journey in Derbyshire and Staffordshire, the
Stonyshire and Loamshire of " Adam Bede." At the age
of eight she was sent to a large school at Nuneaton,
kept by Miss Wallington. Here she made acquaintance
with the works of Scott and Charles Lamb, also with the

"History of the Devil" by Defoe. Her copy of this, illustrated by strange pictures, is still preserved at Griff. "The Pilgrim's Progress" and "Rasselas" were also favourite objects of study. The principal governess of the school was Miss Lewis, who remained for many years a devoted friend of George Eliot's. Many of her letters to this lady have been published by Mr. Cross.

The years from twelve to fifteen, most important years of growth, were spent at a school at Coventry, kept by two sisters, daughters of a Baptist minister named Franklin. The house still stands as No 48 of Little Park Street, in the centre of the town, near St. Michael's Church. The younger sister, Miss Rebecca Franklin, was a woman of rare attainments, a beautiful writer, remarkable for the elegance and correctness of her speech. It was to her that George Eliot owed that preciseness of phrase and delivery which afterwards distinguished her; and from her perhaps she acquired her gift of English style, which beginning with formal primness, not devoid of affectation, acquired afterwards the genial fulness of imagination and diction which has placed her in the first rank of English writers. The tone of the school was deeply Evangelical. Prayer meetings were in vogue among the pupils. Here, as in her own family, she was surrounded by those strong religious influences of a Calvinistic type which so powerfully affected her mind in its first development. I remember her once telling me, when speaking of the attitude which she then held towards Christianity, how her early years had been passed amongst surroundings of the strictest orthodoxy. She left school in December, 1835, being called home by the illness of her mother, who died in the following summer. Not long afterwards her sister married, and the charge of the household and the farm devolved upon George Eliot. She became an adept at butter-making, and she used to declare in later years that her right hand was broader than her left from the amount of butter which she had made in her youth. She writes to Miss Lewis with fingers tremulous from the boiling of currant jelly, and again with a stupid, drowsy sensation produced by "standing sentinel over damson cheese and a warm stove." At another period sewing is her staple article of commerce with the hard trader Time. Yet she was able to devote a large amount of attention to charitable and intellectual pursuits. She visited the poor and organized clothing clubs. She learnt Italian and German from Signor Brezzi, of Coventry, who often spoke of the marvellous ease with which she acquired languages. She had been the show pianist at Miss Franklin's school, and with developed powers was able to gratify her father's love of music. Her condition at this period is best shown in a letter to Miss Lewis, of September 4, 1839, which also exhibits her innate fondness for the use of scientific metaphor.

"I have lately led so unsettled a life, and have been so desultory in my employments, that my mind, never of the most highly organized genus, is more than usually chaotic; or rather it is like a stratum of conglomerated fragments, that shows here a jaw and rib of some ponderous quadruped, there a delicate alto-relievo of some fern-like plant, tiny shells, and mysterious nondescripts encrusted and united with some unvaried and uninteresting but useful stone.

My mind presents just such an assemblage of disjointed specimens of history, ancient and modern, scraps of poetry picked up from Shakspeare, Cowper, Wordsworth, and Milton ; newspaper topics ; morsels of Addison and Bacon, Latin verbs, geometry, entomology, and chemistry ; Reviews and metaphysics—all arrested and petrified and smothered by the fast-thickening anxiety of actual events, relative anxieties, and household cares and vexations. . . . Remember Michaelmas is coming, and I shall be engaged in matters so nauseating to me that it will be a charity to console me."

She wrote again on November 22nd, her twentieth birthday : " I have emerged from the slough of domestic troubles, or rather, to speak quite clearly, *malheurs de cuisine.*" She now begins to take great interest in the study of Wordsworth, and had before this made her first appearance as an author. She had scribbled prose and poetry from her early childhood, but her earliest known composition is the stanzas printed in the *Christian Observer* for January, 1840, of which the refrain is "Farewell !" They exhibit the defects of her later poetry without the glow of eloquence to which it occasionally rises. She was also busied with preparing a Chart of Ecclesiastical History, a design which was given up when a better one was published. Her mind was drawn early to history, and especially to that form of the study which delights in realizing the life of bygone ages. We find this tendency in her later admiration of Monteil and Riehl. "Romola," the best historical novel ever written, and in the opinion of many the foremost of her works, had its roots deep in the foundation of her mind. The life at Griff, so strange a mixture of the practical and the ideal, was put an end to by her removal to Coventry. Her brother Isaac married ; her father was becoming old and feeble. It seemed natural that the son should succeed to Griff and that the father should retire. So in March, 1841, father and daughter remove to Foleshill, a semi-detached villa just on the outskirts of Coventry. A new life with unexpected developments was to open upon George Eliot.

Her next-door neighbour at Foleshill was Mrs. Pears, who soon grew into the more precious character of a friend. At her house she met for the first time Mr. and Mrs. Bray of Rosehill. He was a wealthy ribbon manufacturer, with a large house in the outskirts of the town. He had at this time published the "Education of the Feelings," and the "Philosophy of Necessity," his most important work. He was a sincere believer in phrenology, and persuaded George Eliot to have her head shaved in order that a caste might be taken of it, which still exists. His wife was the sister of Mr. Charles Hennell, who had published in 1838 "An Inquiry Concerning the Origin of Christianity," a remarkable book, which was translated into German, with a preface by Strauss. There is no doubt that the study of this book produced a profound effect on George Eliot's religious opinions. Her life at this time is thus described by one who must have known it well :—

"In this somewhat now popular neighbourhood she soon became known as a person of more than common interest, and, moreover, as a most devoted daughter, and the excellent manager of her father's household. There was, perhaps, little at first sight which betokened genius in that quiet, gentle-mannered girl with pale grave face, naturally pensive in expression; and ordinary acquaintances regarded her chiefly for the kindness and sympathy which were never wanting to any. But to those with whom, by some un-spoken affinity, her soul could expand, her expressive grey eyes would light up with intense meaning and humour, and the low sweet voice, with its peculiar mannerism of speaking—which, by the way, wore off in after-years—would give utterance to thoughts so rich and singular that converse with Miss Evans, even in those days, made speech with other people seem flat and common. At Foleshill, with ample means and leisure, her real education began. She took lessons in Greek and Latin from the Rev. J. Sheepshanks, then head-master of the Coventry Grammar School, and she acquired French, German, and Italian from Signor Brezzi. An acquaintance with Hebrew was the result of her own unaided efforts. From Mr. Simms, the veteran organist of St. Michael's, Coventry, she received lessons in music, although it was her own fine musical sense which made her in after-years an admirable pianoforte player. Nothing once learned escaped her marvellous memory ; and her keen sympathy with all human feelings, in which lay the secret of her power of discriminating character, caused a constant fund of knowledge to flow into her treasurehouse from the social world around her. In Mr. Bray's family she found sympathy with her ardent love of knowledge, and with the more enlightened views that had begun to supplant those under which (as she described it) her spirit had been grievously burdened. Emerson, Froude, George Combe, Roberts, Mackay, and many other men of mark were at various times guests at Mr. Bray's house at Rosehill, while Miss Evans was there either as an inmate or occasional visitor ; and many a time might have been seen, pacing up and down the lawn, or grouped under an old acacia, men of thought and research, discussing all things in heaven and earth, and listening with marked attention when one gentle woman's voice was heard to utter what they were quite sure had been well matured before the lips opened. Few, if any, could feel themselves her superior in general intelli-gence, and it was amusing one day to see the amazement of a certain doctor, who, venturing on a quotation from Epictetus to an unas-suming young lady, was, with modest politeness, corrected in his Greek by his feminine auditor. One real characteristic belonged to her which gave a peculiar charm to her conversation. She had no petty egotism, no spirit of contradiction. She never talked for effect. A happy thought well expressed filled her with delight ; in a moment she would seize the point and improve upon it—so that common people began to feel themselves wise in her presence, and perhaps years after she would remind them, to their pride and surprise, of the good things they had said." [1]

The friendship with the Brays bore such speedy fruit that at the end of 1841 she determined to give up going to church. This nearly produced a rupture with her father, who threatened to leave Foleshill and live with his married daughter, while Miss Evans was to remove to Leamington and to support herself by teaching. After a painful struggle of two months George Eliot went to stay with her brother at the old house of Griff, where she was treated with every delicacy and consideration. She writes, however—"I do not intend to remain here longer than three weeks, or, at the very farthest, a month; and if I am not then recalled, I shall write for definite directions. I must have a *home*, not a visiting place." Before the close of the month matters were arranged. Her father received her back again, and she went to church as before. This collision with her father, which she thought might have been avoided, caused her regret to the end of her life.

Six months later she wrote to her friend, Miss Sara Hennell, her views on the subject of conformity, which showed how her deep-seated charity and sympathy with others made her less inclined to dwell on the value of her individual convictions. She tells her that the first impulse of a young and ingenuous mind is to withhold

[1] *Pall Mall Budget*, December 31, 1880.

the slightest sanction from all that contains even a mixture of supposed error ; that the soul just liberated from the wretched giant's bed of dogmas on which it has been racked and stretched ever since it began to think has a feeling of exultation and strong hope, which prompts it to proselytize others.   But years bring reflection.   Speculative truth begins to appear but a shadow of individual minds, and the truth of feeling is seen to be the only universal bond of union.   Intellectual errors cannot be wrenched away from the living body without destroying vitality.   The only safe revolution for individuals, as for nations, is that which arises from the wants which their own progress has generated.   It is the quackery of infidelity to suppose that it has a nostrum for all mankind, and to say to all and singular —"Swallow my opinions, and you shall be whole."   The best and the only way of fulfilling our mission is to sow good seed in good, that is, in prepared ground, and not to root up tares where we must inevitably gather all the wheat with them.   This conviction remained with her to the end of her life.   It induced her to say nothing in her books which could hurt the feelings of a single believing soul.   "The great thing to teach," she once wrote to me, " is reverence—reverence for the hard-won inheritance of the ages."

In 1842 a number of friends and guests of Mr. Joseph Parkes, the well-known Parliamentary agent of the Liberal party, determined that the best way of helping on the development of free religious thought in England was to translate the " Leben Jesu " of Strauss—a book of unsparing destructive criticism of the sources of the life of Christ. Funds were subscribed for the purpose, and Mr. Hennell undertook to find a translator. The work was entrusted to Miss Brabant, the daughter of Dr. Brabant, of Devizes, a lady who, as Mrs. Call, still preserves in all their freshness the memories of that distinguished circle. When the translation had reached to page 218 of vol. i. it was interrupted by the marriage of Miss Brabant to Mr. Hennell; and Miss Evans, who had met Miss Brabant in an excursion to Tenby, undertook to complete the work. It occupied her about two years and a quarter, and had an important effect on her intellectual development. She told me that her greatest difficulty was to find the exact English equivalents for German particles. The training thus received, laborious and even repulsive as it was at the time, must have been analogous to that which is derived from the minute study of the classics. It exercised her mind in scholarship, made it easy for her to pursue her reading of Greek literature, and formed the habit of piercing into the depths of an author's meaning, which is the characteristic of the scholar. " I can never," she once said to me, "understand anything of a Greek writer until I have come to comprehend every word "—a slow and laborious process,—" whereas George," she added somewhat archly, " can tell the meaning at a glance." It is strange that in the progress of the translation she should complain of the illegibility of a handwriting which was at a later period such a marvel of beauty and neatness. The money for printing the book was only obtained with difficulty, and Miss Evans received a paltry sum for her trouble. Strauss was thoroughly satisfied with the

English dress which his work had assumed, and a competent reviewer not only praised the easy, perspicuous,
idiomatic, and harmonious form of the English style, but
declared the rendering to be word for word, thought for
thought, and sentence for sentence.

It is only natural to find George Eliot at last dissatisfied with the purely negative character of the work
in which she was occupied. She fairly broke down at
the account of the Crucifixion and the Resurrection, and
of the bursting asunder of Judas. She describes herself
as Strauss-sick—it makes her ill dissecting the beautiful story of the Crucifixion, and only the sight of
"the Christ image and picture" makes her endure it. In
her study at Foleshill stood a biscuit copy of Thorwald-
sen's grand conception of Christ, and on this she was
wont to gaze for inspiration and comfort, just as in later
years a cast of the head of the Melian Asclepius stood
before her writing-table at the Priory to lift her from
thoughts of the modern world. The remorseless analysis
of the German theologian did not prevent her from still
feeling the beauty of the meeting at Emmaüs, so "universal
in its significance." "The soul that has hopelessly followed
Jesus—its impersonation of the highest and the best—
all in despondency; its thoughts all refuted, its dreams
all dissipated! Then comes another Jesus—another,
but the same — the same highest and best, only
chastened—crucified instead of triumphant—and the
soul learns that this is the true way to conquest and
glory. And then there is the burning of the heart, which
assures that 'this was the Lord!'—that this is the inspiration from above—the true comforter that leads unto

truth." The "Life of Jesus" was published on June 15, 1846, and it is satisfactory to know that every copy of the work was eventually sold.

During this labour she had been greatly saddened by the failing health of her father, who was now advanced in years. In July, 1846, when they were staying at Dover, unmistakable signs of impending dissolution appeared, although the end did not come until three years later. During this period she was cheered by new friendships, and the letters to Miss Mary Sibree, now Mrs. Cash, and her brother John, contain sentences which are worthy to be numbered amongst her wise, witty, and tender sayings—

"Do not go to old people as oracles on matters which date later than their thirty-fifth year. . . . Love, cherish, and venerate the old ; but never imagine that a worn-out, dried-up organization can be so rich in inspiration as one which is full fraught with life and energy. . . . No mind that has any *real* life is a mere echo of another. If the perfect unison comes occasionally, as in music, it enhances the harmonies. It is like a diffusion or expansion of one's own life, to be assured that its vibrations are repeated in another, and words are the media of those vibrations. Is not the universe itself a perpetual utterance of the one Being? . . . Take long doses of *dolce far niente*, and be in no great hurry about anything in this 'varsal world. Do we not commit ourselves to sleep and so resign all care for ourselves every night, lay ourselves gently on the bosom of nature and God ?"

Other letters are curious when considered in reference to her future work and life. The future author of "The Spanish Gypsy" and "Daniel Deronda" speaks of the fellowship of race as an inferior impulse which must ultimately be superseded. She declares that the Gentile nature kicks most resolutely against any assumption of

superiority in the Jews, and is almost ready to echo
Voltaire's vituperation—

" I bow to the supremacy of Hebrew poetry, but much of their
early mythology, and almost all their history, is utterly revolting.
Their stock has produced a Moses and a Jesus; but Moses was
impregnated with Egyptian philosophy, and Jesus is venerated and
adored by us only for that wherein He transcended or resisted Judaism.
. . . Everything specifically Jewish is of a low grade."

In another letter she says that the older the world gets,
originality becomes less possible, and that genius which
is deterred from describing highly-wrought agony or
ecstatic sorrow will probably turn itself to the gentler
emotions. This throws great light on the development
of her art. Once again, in an aspiration soon to be gratified, she longs for "the bliss of having a very high attic
in a romantic continental town such as Geneva, far away
from morning callers, dinners, and decencies, and then to
pause for a year to think *de omnibus rebus, et quibusdam
aliis*, and then return to life, and work for poor stricken
humanity and never think of self again."

The constant care of her father produced great depression. She dwells in "Grief Castle, on the Ruins of
Gloom, in the Valley of Dolour." She is like a poor
pebble left entangled among slimy weeds, which hears
from afar the rushing of the blessed torrent, and rejoices
that it is there to bathe and brighten other pebbles less
unworthy of the polishing. Her life is a perpetual nightmare, always haunted by something to be done which
she has never the time or rather the energy to do. To
steady her mind she begins a translation of the " Trac-

tatus Theologico-Politicus" of Spinoza. She sat for hours by her father's side, and never was a patient more admirably and thoroughly cared for. At last the end came. He died in the night of May 31, 1849. "What shall I be without my father!" she cried. "It will seem as if a part of my moral nature were gone."

It happened, fortunately, that the bereaved daughter was soon able to seek the best remedy for mental suffering in a foreign tour. She left England a week after her father's funeral, and in the company of the Brays, went first to the South of France, then to Nice, Genoa, and Milan; and then returning northwards by the way of Como, Maggiore, and the Simplon, she went to Chamouni by the valley of the Rhone, and so passed to Geneva. No letter or diary is published relating to this first foreign tour. Her nerves were so shattered that it is said she could not bear the precipitous slopes even of the carriage passes, and the time of year must have been too late for Italy and too early for Switzerland. At Geneva she determined to remain, and spent there eight happy months. Little is known of her studies and occupation during this important time. All great natures require a period of solitude and rest, of self-collection and self-inspiration for the fulfilment of their missions. The quiet and repose of the Genevan sojourn mark the transition from a period of feverish and fitful growth to one of consciousness of power, and a determination of the best means to reveal herself to the world. Although alone she met with kind and sympathetic friends. During August and September she stayed at the Campagne Plongeon, a boarding-house just outside the town, nestling amongst trees. In October she took lodgings in the house of M. Albert Durade, 107, Rue des Chanoines.[1] M. Durade was an artist, and his portrait of George Eliot is one of the most precious relics of this period. He was also a musician, and a man of great refinement of character. He was a little man with a humped back, and may have suggested Philip Wakem. Madame Durade, with "less of genius and more of cleverness," treated her English guest like a mother. "My want of health," she writes in December, "has obliged me to renounce all application. I take walks, play on the piano, read Voltaire, talk to my friends, and just take a dose of mathematics every day to prevent my brain from becoming quite soft." In another letter she tells the Brays, "I breakfast in my own room at half-past eight, lunch at half-past twelve, and dine at five or a little after, and take tea at eight. From the tea-table I have gone into the salon and chatted until bed-time." Her letters are full of affection for the friends she has left behind her. "My heart ties are not loosened by distance . . . and when I think of my loved ones or those to whom I can be a comforter, a help, I long to be with them again." Otherwise she only thought with a shudder of returning to England. It appeared to her as a land of gloom, of *ennui*, of platitude. "But in the midst of all this it is the land of duty and affection, and the only ardent hope I have for my future life is to have given to

[1] Her room, still shown, is on the second floor of what is now 18, Rue de la Pélisserie. It has a bed in an alcove, and two windows looking down the Rue Calvin. It is approached by a steep, stone winding staircase.

me some woman's duty—some possibility of devoting
myself where I may see a daily result of pure calm
blessedness in the life of another." The severe winter
of Geneva tried her much, and she suffered from frequent
headaches; yet she was able to attend the lectures of
Professor de la Rive on Experimental Physics. In
the middle of March she left Geneva, accompanied by
M. Durade. They had to cross the Jura in sledges,
and suffered terribly from the cold. Arriving in London
on March 23rd, she went straight to Rosehill, and must
have heard at once of the possibility of her lodging at Mr.
Chapman's house in London, a plan which she afterwards carried out. She visited her brother at Griff, and
her sister, Mrs. Clarke, at Meriden. But these did not
satisfy her. "Oh! the dismal weather," she writes, "and
the dismal country, and the dismal people. It was
some envious demon that drove me across the Jura."
It would seem that the companionship of Adam Bede
and Mrs. Poyser was not as pleasant as the recollection
of them in a suburban villa. In May she returned to
Rosehill again, and stayed there till November. There she
wrote a review of Mackay's "Progress of the Intellect,"
which appeared in the *Westminster Review* for January,
1851. This has not been reprinted, as by her express
wish no writings of hers have been republished which
appeared earlier than 1857. It contains, however, an
independent statement of the views at which she had
then arrived with regard to the progressive education of
the human race. The success of this article seems to
have involved her more completely in the enterprize
which Mr. Chapman was then inaugurating,—the starting

of the *Westminster Review* under new auspices. She
took part in drawing up the prospectus of the new journal,
and in September went to live at Mr. Chapman's house,
with the definite post of assistant editor.

In this capacity the choice and arrangement of
articles fell principally on her shoulders. She was thus
brought into close contact with many of the most distinguished among the advanced thinkers and writers of
the day, but she had an opportunity of meeting a more
general circle in the fortnightly gatherings which were
held at Mr. Chapman's house. Amongst her first friends
made in this manner was Mr. Herbert Spencer, with whom
she became extremely intimate. He takes her, with Mr.
Chapman, to the theatre and to the opera. She writes
of him : " We have agreed that there is no reason why
we should not have as much of each other's society as
we like. He is a good, delightful creature, and I always
feel better for being with him." Again, " My brightest
spot, next to my love of *old* friends, is the deliciously
calm *new* friendship that Herbert Spencer gives me.
We see each other every day, and have a delightful
camaraderie in everything." Mr. Spencer is thus the
best living repository of the traditions of that period,
which some day he may perhaps give to the world. He
it was who first discovered that the genius of George
Eliot lay in writing romance. He had always recommended her to adopt this course, and one day when
visiting at Park Shot, George Lewes told him that she
had begun, and showed him the manuscript of the
" Scenes of Clerical Life." A letter to the Brays, written in
November, 1852, gives a vivid idea of her occupations—

3

"I will just tell you how it was last Saturday, and that will give you an idea of my days. My task was to read an article of Greg's in the *North British*, on Taxation, a heap of newspaper articles, and all that J. S. Mill says on the same subject. When I had got some way into this *magnum mare*, in comes Mr. Chapman, with a thick German volume. 'Will you read enough of this to give me your opinion of it?' Then of course I must have a walk after lunch, and when I had set down again, thinking that I had two clear hours before dinner, rap at the door, Mr. Lewes, who, of course, sits talking till the second bell rings. After dinner another visitor, and so behold me, at 11 p.m., still so very far at sea on the subject of Taxation, but too tired to keep my eyes open."

George Henry Lewes, whose name occurs in the last quotation, and who was destined to have so important an effect upon her life, was at this time a well-known figure in London literary circles. Coming to London in 1839, and contributing to a large number of journals, he had written a "Biographical History of Philosophy," which, beginning in two small volumes, afterwards expanded into two portly tomes. He had published two novels, a tragedy, and a "Life of Robespierre." His bright eyes, his long black hair, his plain and strongly marked features, are well known to many now living, who also remember his ready wit, his admirable hospitality, his exquisite French, and his never-failing kindness. George Eliot, when she first met him, called him a Mirabeau in miniature. He was afterwards formally introduced to her by Herbert Spencer, and seems rapidly to have gained the first place in her intimacy. With the exception of a review of Carlyle's "Life of Sterling," in January, 1852, she did not contribute anything of her own to the *Westminster* until the article on

"Women in France: Madame de Sablé," in October, 1854. This was followed by " Evangelical Teaching : Dr. Cumming," in October, 1855; "German Wit : Heinrich Heine," in January, 1856; "Silly Novels by Lady Novelists," October, 1856; " The Natural History of German Life ; a review of Riehl," in July, 1856 ; and " Worldliness and Other-worldliness : the Poetry of Young," in January, 1857. The last five of these, with the exception of the "Silly Novels," have been reprinted in her works. Yet this is full of humour and sarcasm, and perhaps for that reason the strong moral hold which she always kept over her tongue prevented her from reproducing it. It contains also a sketch of English country life, which announces the future author of " Adam Bede." She complains of the want of reality with which peasant life is commonly treated in art, and goes on to remark—

" The notion that peasants are joyous, that the typical moment to represent a man in a smock frock is when he is cracking a joke and showing a row of sound teeth, that cottage matrons are usually buxom, and village children necessarily rosy and merry, are prejudices difficult to dislodge from the artistic mind which takes for its subjects such literature instead of life. Idyllic ploughmen are jocund when they drive their team afield ; idyllic shepherds make bashful love under hawthorn bushes ; idyllic villagers dance in the chequered shade, and refresh themselves most immoderately with spicy nut-brown ale. But no one who has seen much of actual ploughmen thinks them jocund, no one who is well acquainted with the English peasantry can pronounce them merry. The slow gaze, in which no sense of beauty beams, no humour twinkles; the slow utterance, and the heavy, slouching walk, remind one rather of that melancholy animal the camel, than of the sturdy countryman with striped stockings, red waistcoat, and hat aside, who represents the traditional English peasant. That delicious

effervescence of mind which we call fun has no equivalent for the
northern peasant, except tipsy revelry ; the only realm of fancy and
imagination for the English clown exists at the bottom of the third
quart pot."

Her attack on Dr. Cumming is very scathing:

"Given a man with a moderate intellect, a moral standard not
higher than the average, some rhetorical affluence, and great glib-
ness of speech, which is the career in which, without aid of birth or
money, he may most easily obtain power and reputation in English
society ? Where is that Goshen of intellectual mediocrity, in which
a smattering of science and learning will pass for profound instruction, where platitudes will be accepted as wisdom, bigoted manners
as holy zeal, unctuous egotism as God-given piety ! Let such a
man become an evangelical preacher ; he will then find it possible
to reconcile such ability with great ambition, superficial knowledge with the prestige of erudition, a middling *morale* with a high
reputation for sanctity. Let him show practical extremes, and be
ultra in what is only purely theoretic. Let him be stringent in
predestination, but latitudinarian in fasting ; unflinching in insisting
on the eternity of punishment, but diffident of curtailing the sub-
stantial comforts of time ; ardent and imaginative on the pre-
millenial advent of Christ, but cold and cautious towards every
other infringement of the *status quo*. . . . Above all, let him set up
as an interpreter of prophecy, rival ' Moore's Almanack ' in the
prediction of political events, trebling the interest of hearers who
are but moderately spiritual by showing them how the Holy Spirit
has dictated problems and charades for their benefit, and how, if
they are ingenious enough to solve them, they may have their
Christian graces nourished by learning precisely to whom they may
point as the ' man that had eyes,' the ' lying prophet,' and the ' un-
clean spirits.' In this way he will draw men to him by the strong
cords of their passions, made reason-proof by being baptized by the
name of piety. In this way he may gain a metropolitan pulpit ; the
avenues to his church will be as crowded as the passages to the
opera ; he has but to print his prophetic sermons, and bind them in
lilac and gold, and they will adorn the drawing-room table of all

Evangelical ladies, who will regard as a sort of pious ' light
reading' the demonstration that the prophecy of the locusts, whose
sting is in their tail, is fulfilled in the fact of the Turkish commander
having taken a horse's tail for his standard; and that the French
are the very frogs predicted in the Revelation."

In the mean time the intimacy with Mr. Lewes was
growing gradually stronger. She writes in the spring of
1853 : "I am in for loads of work next quarter, but
I shall not tell you what I am going to do. . . . Lewes,
as always, genial and amusing. He has quite won my
liking, in spite of myself." And a month later, " People
are very good to me. Mr. Lewes especially is kind
and attentive, and has quite won my regard, after having
had a good deal of my vituperation. Like a few other
people in the world, he is much better than he seems.
A man of heart and conscience wearing a mask of
flippancy." After a summer spent at St. Leonards, she
determines to leave Mr. Chapman's house, and takes
lodgings on the ground floor of No. 21, Cambridge
Street, Hyde Park. It was this change of lodgings, and
not the journey to Weimar, as is generally supposed,
which marked the commencement of the union with
Mr. Lewes. This new life had a favourable effect upon
her health. She writes on her thirty-fourth birthday :
"I begin this year more happily than I have done
most years of my life. . . . We *may* both find ourselves
at the end of the year going faster to the hell of conscious moral and intellectual weakness. Still there is
a possibility—even a probability—the other way." She
now makes arrangements for surrendering the editorship
of the *Westminster Review.* She translates Feuerbach's

"Essence of Christianity," and announces a book on "The Idea of a Future Life," which, however, was never published, and perhaps never written. Mr. Lewes was at this time literary editor of the *Leader*, a paper far in advance of its age, the proprietor of which, Mr. Edward Pigott, Her Majesty's inspector of plays, still lives to enjoy the respect and affection of all who know him. Mr. Lewes falls ill, George Eliot has to nurse him, and to do his work for the *Leader*. At last the translation of Feuerbach is published, and the workman is free to depart.

She writes to Miss Hennell on July 10th: "I shall soon send you a good-bye, for I am preparing to go abroad (?) " And she writes ten days later :

"Dear Friends,—all three—I have only time to say good-bye, and God bless you. *Poste Restante*, Weimar, for the next six weeks, and afterwards Berlin.
"Ever your loving and grateful
"Marian."

On that very day she left London for Antwerp with Mr. Lewes, and the *Leader* found itself unexpectedly without an editor.

The union of George Eliot with George Henry Lewes was the most important event in her life. It was a true marriage, undertaken with all the deliberation and solemnity with which such a step should be contemplated. She had already written in her translation of Feuerbach (p. 268), "a marriage, the bond of which is merely an external restriction, not the voluntary, contented self-restriction of love ; in short, a marriage which is not spontaneously concluded, spontaneously willed, self-sufficing, is not a

true marriage, and therefore not a truly moral marriage."
This union was a source of strength and happiness to
both the parties who contracted it.   The dedications
of the manuscript of each succeeding novel declare
in varying language how her beloved husband was
the only source of all her insight, and all her strength.
She was, I have said, of a nature which needed some
one to lean upon, and he worshipped and guarded
her with a never-failing tenderness of affection. " Polly,"
as he used to call her, was in his eyes at once the
greatest of living geniuses, and the best and the most
loveable of women.   Without his insight into literary
faculty, and his sustaining sympathy, it is doubtful
whether she would have produced the writings which
have made her fame, and which were only born at the cost
of so much travail and self-renunciation.   It is needless
to gratify a morbid curiosity as to the origin or development of the relations between them.   Miss Evans fell
in love with Lewes as she had fallen in love with
others, for she had a strong, passionate nature.   She was
once, at a period which I have not been able to verify,
engaged to an artist whose subsequent career made it
a happiness to her that the marriage was never carried
out.   Perhaps some of the more passionate scenes in
her novels are transcripts from her own experiences.
Lewes was evidently subdued by her large commanding
nature, and her burning power of sympathy.   Marriage
in the ordinary sense was impossible, as Lewes's wife
was still alive, and circumstances which need not be
here related had made a divorce impracticable. There was
some talk at a later period of marriage abroad, but it

was never put into effect. A fable was invented by society
that Mrs. Lewes was dead, but it had no foundation.
The travellers went to Weimar as Mr. Lewes and Miss
Evans, and it is believed that it was only by the advice
of Mr. Arthur Helps, who accompanied them on the
second visit to Ettersburg, on August 29th, that they
determined thenceforth to call themselves man and wife.
The Court of Weimar did not at first understand the relationship, and it was not until just before their departure
from Weimar that Lewes was invited to the Palace,
and charmed the ducal circle by the fascination of his
conversation.

Of the eight months they spent abroad, three were
passed at Weimar, and five at Berlin. They were days
of unclouded happiness and steady work. Indeed, it
is difficult to understand why George Eliot, who was
always most happy and most productive under the
circumstances of foreign life, should have lived so much
in England, except that her husband was a confirmed
Londoner. Their lodgings at Weimar were at the
corner of a short street leading out of the Market Place,
not far from the Park. They visited Ilmenau, afterwards a favourite resort of George Eliot's. They met
Strauss at Cologne, and Liszt at Weimar. At Berlin
they moved more freely among literary circles. They
were received kindly by Varnhagen von Ense ; they delighted in the society of Rauch the sculptor, and in the
congenial companionship of Adolf Stahr and Fanny
Lewald. "They were very happy months," she says, "we
spent at Berlin, in spite of the bitter cold which came on
in January, and lasted almost till we left. How we used

to rejoice in the idea of our warm room and coffee as
we battled our way from dinner against the wind and
snow ! Then came the delightful long evenings, in which
we read Shakspeare, Goethe, Heine, and Macaulay,
with German *Pfefferkuchen* and *Semmels* at the end
to complete the *noctes cenæque deûm.*" They dined at
the Hôtel de l'Europe, and read books at table ! They
walked at night along the Linden, and over the bridge
towards the Schloss. The time was well spent. While
Lewes worked at his Life of Goethe, in which he had the
benefit of her criticisms, she reviewed Victor Cousin's
" Madame de Sablé " and Vehse's "Court of Austria,"
besides nearly finishing the translation of Spinoza's
"Ethics." Her power of reading out aloud was very
great, her natural gifts having been developed by the prac-
tice she had in reading to her father. She could read a
German book out aloud for three or four hours without
tiring, and her elocution was exquisite. On March 13,
1855, they arrived at the Lord Warden Hotel, at Dover,
to take up the full responsibility of a married couple.
Perhaps in the view of the coming struggles attendant
upon fame and triumph, this eight months' sojourn was
the brightest spot in their lives.

CHAPTER II.

FROM her return to England, in March, 1855, George Eliot began the life which she continued to the day of her death, that of a married woman of letters, working hard for her living, endeavouring to fulfil the duties of her vocation; performing with conscientious love and devotion the part of a wife and mother. For a short time she and her husband had lodgings at East Sheen, but afterwards removed to 8, Park Shot, Richmond, where they remained for three years. Here they only had apartments. Their piano overhead was likely to disturb the clerical gentleman below, and the scratching of Lewes' pen grated on his wife's nerves as she worked in the same room. It was important that they should both obtain employment. George Eliot was engaged to write the article on Belles Lettres for the *Westminster Review*, and also articles for the *Leader*, neither, we fear, very remunerative. An article, published in *Fraser*, April, 1855, on Weimar and its celebrities, is really rather poor. It is an attempt to be popular, and it ends in being commonplace. It shows nothing of the power which was exhibited in the article on Dr. Cumming, which occupied from June 13th to August 24th of this year. Lewes'

"Life of Goethe" was published and had a large sale. It is still regarded, even in Germany, as the classical life of Goethe. It is a good introduction to the study of the German poet for those who have not before approached him, but there are many sides of Goethe with which it does not deal, and it becomes every year less satisfactory from the growth of knowledge. Lewes had determined to exchange literature for those studies which he believed to be more especially his own, the inquiry into the sources of animal life, and through life into the sources of mind. This led to expeditions to the sea-side—to Ilfracombe, Jersey, and Tenby—with the object of pursuing these researches. It also led to George Eliot, through sympathy with her husband's studies, paying great attention to science, and perhaps exaggerating the use of scientific metaphor which, natural to her from the first, became more habitual as years went on. In the midst of these articles a more permanent occupation was the translation of Spinoza's "Ethics." All this must have been hard work. Lewes, at the age of thirty-nine, had not amassed much money from his varied labours ; while his wife only had a small allowance from her father's estate. Besides, his three boys were growing up, and had to be educated. "I keep the purse," she writes, "and dole out sovereigns with all the pangs of a miser. In fact, if you were to feel my bump of acquisitiveness, I dare say you would find it in a state of inflammation, like the 'veneration' of that clergyman to whom Mr. Donovan said, 'Sir, you have recently been engaged in prayer.'"

In May, 1856, George Eliot, on her way to Ilfracombe, paid her first visit to Windsor, an experience which she renewed some ten years later as my guest. At Ilfracombe she accompanied Lewes in his search for marine specimens, and her recollections are full of uncouth Latin names, in which she did her best to take an interest. More to her taste evidently were the shifting and indescribable beauties of an English landscape. To these months belong the essay on Young's "Night Thoughts," "Worldliness and Other-worldliness," perhaps the greatest of her productions in this line, and the review of Riehl, both of which have been reprinted. She was, however, already thinking of adopting that form of composition by which her great reputation was to be attained. She writes in her journal, under the date July 20, 1856, " I am anxious to begin my fiction writing, and so am not inclined to undertake an article that will give me much trouble." And, again, on August 18th, while walking with Lewes in Kew Park, she talked to him of her novel. At this time she was writing her article on " Silly Novels by Lady Novelists," which she seems to have begun from a course of reading on the subject that then most interested her, and with a view of guarding herself from the faults which others had committed in similar enterprizes.

The actual genesis of the " Scenes of Clerical Life " can only be fitly told in her own words :—

"September 1856 made a new era in my life, for it was then I began to write fiction. It had always been a vague dream of mine that some time or other I might write a novel ; and my shadowy conception of what the novel was to be, varied, of course, from one epoch of my life to another. But I never went further towards the actual writing of the novel than an introductory chapter

describing a Staffordshire village and the life of the neighbouring
farm-houses; and as the years passed on I lost any hope that I
should ever be able to write a novel, just as I desponded about
everything else in my future life. I always thought I was deficient
in dramatic power, both of construction and dialogue, but I felt
I should be at my ease in the descriptive parts of a novel. My
'introductory chapter' was pure description, though there were
good materials in it for dramatic presentation. It happened to be
among the papers I had with me in Germany, and one evening at
Berlin something led me to read it to George. He was struck with
it as a bit of concrete description, and it suggested to him the
possibility of my being able to write a novel, though he distrusted
—indeed disbelieved in—my possession of any dramatic power.
Still he began to think that I might as well try some time what I
could do in fiction; and by and by when we came back to England,
and I had greater success than he ever expected in other kinds of
writing, his impression that it was worth while to see how far my
mental power would go towards the production of a novel, was
strengthened. He began to say very positively, 'You must try and
write a story,' and when we were at Tenby he urged me to begin at
once. I deferred it, however, after my usual fashion with work
that does not present itself as an absolute duty. But one morning,
as I was thinking what should be the subject of my first story, my
thoughts merged themselves into a dreamy doze, and I imagined
myself writing a story, of which the title was, 'The Sad Fortunes
of the Reverend Amos Barton.' I was soon wide awake again and
told G. He said, 'Oh, what a capital title!' and from that time
I had settled in my mind that this should be my first story.
George used to say, 'It may be a failure — it may be that you
are unable to write fiction. Or perhaps it may be just good
enough to warrant you trying again.' Again, 'You may write a
chef-d œuvre at once—there's no telling.' But his prevalent impression was, that though I could hardly write a *poor* novel, my
effort would want the highest quality of fiction—dramatic presentation. He used to say, 'You have wit, description, and philosophy
—those go a good way towards the production of a novel. It is
worth while for you to try the experiment.'

"We determined that if my story turned out good enough, we

would send it to Blackwood ; but G. thought the more probable result was that I should have to lay it aside and try again.

"But when we returned to Richmond, I had to write my article on 'Silly Novels,' and my review of Contemporary Literature for the *Westminster*, so that I did not begin my story till September 22. After I had begun it, as we were walking in the park, I mentioned to G. that I had thought of the plan of writing a series of stories, containing sketches drawn from my own observations of the clergy, and calling them 'Scenes from Clerical Life,' opening with 'Amos Barton.'   He at once accepted the notion as a good one—fresh and striking ; and about a week afterwards, when I read him the first part of ' Amos,' he had no longer any doubt about my ability to carry out the plan.   The scene at Cross Farm, he said, satisfied him that I had the very element he had been doubtful about—it was clear that I could write good dialogue. There still remained the question whether I could command any pathos ; and that was to be decided by the mode in which I treated Milly's death.   One night G. went to town on purpose to leave me a quiet evening for writing it.   I wrote the chapter from the news brought by the shepherd to Mrs. Hackit, to the moment when Amos is dragged from the bedside, and I read it to G. when he came home.   We both cried over it, and then he came up to me and kissed me, saying, ' I think your pathos is better than your fun.' "

" Amos Barton " was written between September 22, and November 5, 1856. It was sent by Lewes to Mr. Blackwood with a commendatory letter and was received. The publisher was very cautious, but his criticisms do not seem to be of great value. He congratulates George Eliot on being " worthy of print and pay." Misunderstanding a phrase of Lewes', he says, " I am glad that your friend is, as I supposed, a clergyman. Such a subject is best in clerical hands, and some of the pleasantest and least prejudiced correspondents I have ever had are English clergymen." George Eliot a clergyman ! Heaven save

the mark! The publisher warmed in his appreciation
when he saw the story in print. He sent a cheque for
fifty guineas, and added, " It is a long time since I have
read anything so fresh, so humorous, and so touching.
The style is capital, conveying so much in so few
words." He also made overtures for republishing the
series. The story soon attracted attention. Albert
Smith has the credit of sounding the first note of
approval.

The first of the "Scenes of Clerical Life" was
drawn, like all other good art, from personal experience.
Shepperton Church is Chilvers Coton, a suburb of
Nuneaton. In this church Mary Ann Evans was baptized, and she attended it during the whole of her
residence at Griff. It stands close to the Vicarage. The
"little flight of steps, with their wooden rail running
up the outer wall and leading to the children's gallery,"
still exists, and has not been removed in the restoration
of the church. This restoration took place when George
Eliot was fifteen and must have made a deep impression
upon her mind. The Vicarage is a pleasant-looking,
old-fashioned house, with a pretty garden in front, and
everything around neat and well ordered. The Rev.
Amos Barton was in reality the Rev. John Gwyther, B.A.,
and Milly Barton was his wife Emma. Mrs. Hackit
is supposed to be a sketch of George Eliot's mother.
The story told by George Eliot, the struggle of the
curate's family to live, the taking of a foreign lady
into the family, the death of Mrs. Gwyther, were subjects
of common conversation in the neighbourhood during
George Eliot's girlhood, and if Mrs. Evans really attended

at Milly's death-bed there is a strong reason for her daughter knowing all about it. Indeed, Emma Gwyther did not die till 1836, so that George Eliot probably knew her personally. The story shows the full strength of George Eliot's genius mixed with some weaknesses which disappeared at a later period. The dialogue is admirably dramatic. Her power of objective representation was fully grown from the first. The homely wit so apparent in "Adam Bede" here shows itself as a new force in literature. "You're like the wood-pigeon: it says do—do—do all day, and never sets about any work itself." "When he tries to preach without book he rambles about and doesn't stick to his text; and every now and then he flounders about like a sheep that has cast itself, and can't get on its legs again." On the other hand, the Greek quotation at the end of chapter iv. is not very appropriate, and is probably inserted to keep up the idea that the writer is a man. The opening reflections of chapter v., a defence of uninteresting characters, are too obviously an imitation of Walter Scott, and are rather long in proportion to the story; and the same might be said of other paragraphs. Nanny, however, the servant, is a most life-like creature, and her conversation is as true and racy as any which George Eliot ever penned. It is needless to praise the pathos of Milly's death, not less remarkable for its intense feeling than for its strong self-repression. The criticism of Mr. Blackwood curtailed the conclusion of the story, which related the fate of the children. Most readers would prefer that it had been left in its original state.

"Mr. Gilfil's Love-Story," begun immediately after the conclusion of "Amos Barton," was finished in the Scilly Islands, in May, 1857. It also is laid amongst scenes of her early recollections, although it is not known how far the plot is based on fact. The introduction of the Italian element, which the writer could only have learnt superficially from travel, points to the coming "Romola." It is also remarkable that these first two stories depend for their interest on the incongruity between English and foreign views of life and conduct. Cheverell Manor is Arbury Hall, in the grounds of which George Eliot was born. Sir Christopher Cheverell is Sir Roger Newdigate, a family already commemorated by the Oldinports of "Amos Barton." He rebuilt and redecorated his ancient family seat precisely in the manner described in the novel. Maynard Gilfil was the ward of Sir Christopher, who when at Milan had adopted a little Italian orphan girl, and had brought her up at Cheverell. It is said that Sir Roger Newdigate had adopted a village girl with a beautiful voice. Tina, the Italian girl, is destined to be Maynard's wife, whereas she is heart and soul in love with Captain Wybrow, Sir Christopher's heir, whom he wishes to marry to a rich heiress, Miss Archer. Wybrow has no intention of marrying the penniless Italian, but he makes love to her, and excuses himself to his betrothed by alleging Tina's importunity. Tina, furious with passion and jealousy secretes a dagger, she scarcely knows with what object, and going to meet Wybrow in the woods, finds him stretched on the ground dead of heart disease. She runs away, but is recovered and marries Gilfil. She dies within the year and

4

"Maynard Gilfil's love went with her into deep silence for evermore." He sits down in his bare dining-room, whilst in another part of the house, cleaned by his servants once a quarter, is a chamber with an oriel window, with a dainty looking-glass over a dressing-table, 'a faded satin pin-cushion with the pins rusted in it, a scent-bottle and a large green fan lay on the table, and on a dressing-box by the side of the glass was a work-basket and an unfinished baby-cap, yellow with age, lying in it.' "Such was the locked-up chamber in Mr. Gilfil's house, a sort of visible symbol of the secret chamber in his heart, where he had long turned the key on early hopes and early sorrows, shutting up for ever all the passion and the poetry of his life."

The Knebley Church of the story is Astley Church, about a mile from Arbury, topping a hill with a fine view. The ruins of Astley Castle are close by. Here Mr. Gilfil officiated in the afternoon, "in a wonderful little church with a checkered pavement, which had once rung to the iron-tread of military monks, with coats of arms in clusters on the lofty roof, marble warriors and their heads without noses occupying a large proportion of the area, and the twelve apostles, with their heads very much on one side, holding didactic ribbons, painted in fresco on the walls." There is a similar church on a hill at Norbury in Derbyshire, amidst the scenery of "Adam Bede."

The epilogue to "Mr. Gilfil's Love-Story," written on Fortification Hill, Scilly Islands, one sunshiny morning, contains a lovely passage of universal application, which throws a strong light upon George Eliot's philosophy :—

"It is with men as with trees : if you lop off their finest branches, into which they are pouring their young life-juice, the wounds will be healed over with some rough boss, some odd excrescence, and what might have been a grand tree expanding into liberal shade is but a whimsical misshapen trunk. Many an irritating fault, many an unlovely oddity, has come of a hard sorrow, which has crushed and maimed the nature just when it was expanding into plenteous beauty; and the trivial erring life, which we visit with our harsh blame, may be but as the unsteady motion of a man whose best limb is withered."

"Janet's Repentance," the last of the "Scenes," had been begun in the Scilly Islands, on April 18, 1857, but the greater part of it was written in Jersey, where the Leweses had delightful lodgings, at Gorey in the Bay of Granville, within sight of the castle of Montorgueil. "It was a sweet beautiful life we led there. Good creatures the Amys, our host and hostess, with their nice boy and girl, and the little white kid—the family pet. No disagreeable sounds to be heard in the house, no unpleasant qualities to hinder one from feeling perfect love to these simple people." They spent their time in long rambles and long readings ; George Eliot reading aloud "Draper's Physiology" in the "grave evening hours." They dined at five. George Eliot's strength increased in this delicious quiet, and she had fewer interruptions to meet, from headache, than she had experienced since Christmas. She writes to Blackwood on June 2nd : "Lewes seems to have higher expectations from the third story than from either of the preceding ; but I can form no judgment myself, until I have quite finished a thing, and see it aloof from my actual self. I can only go on writing what I feel, and waiting for the proof that I have been able to make others feel." Strangely enough, Blackwood did not like the story. He thought that it dealt too much with clerical matters, and George Eliot proposed that the series should close with No. 2, and that "Janet's Repentance" should be included if the tales were re-published in a volume. The Leweses returned to Park Shot at the end of July, probably for the sake of their children's holidays; and there "Janet's Repentance" was finished on October 9th. "Adam Bede," the thought of which had already begun to burgeon in the author's mind, was begun on October 22nd. She writes in her diary at the former date : "I had meant to carry on the series, and especially I longed to tell the story of the 'Clerical Tutor,' but my annoyance at Blackwood's want of sympathy in the first part (although he came round to admiration at the third part) determined me to close the series and republish them in two volumes." She received £180 for the first edition of the "Scenes of Clerical Life."

"Janet's Repentance" is, again, full of early recollections. Milby is Nuneaton, so-called from a convent of nuns founded in the reign of King Stephen—in later days a flourishing factory town. The main details of the story are said to be based on actual occurrences. Dempster is the representation of a well-known lawyer. The virtues of his wife Janet still live in the recollections of her fellow-townspeople. Mr. Tryan was curate at the Stockingford chapel-of-ease. Mr. Pilgrim was a well-known doctor. Although George Eliot declared that Mr. Tryan was not a portrait of any clergyman living or dead, and was an ideal character, yet it is probable that she frequently introduced into her writings more exact representations of living people than she was herself aware. The name Milby Mill belongs to a corn-mill in the town standing on the River Anker. The "Red Lion" still flourishes as the "Bull." Mr. Pilgrim, the doctor, has all the trace of a real character.

"I have known Mr. Pilgrim discover the most unexpected virtues in a patient seized with a promising illness. A good in-flammation fired his enthusiasm, and a lingering dropsy dissolved him into charity. Gradually, however, as his patients became convalescent, his view of their character became more dispas-sionate. When they could relish mutton-chops he began to admit that they had foibles, and by the time they had swallowed their last dose of tonic he was alive to their most inexcusable faults. '

"Dempster's" House in Church Street, "an old-fash-ioned house with an overhanging upper storey," still exists. "Outside it had a face of rough stucco, and casement windows with green panes and shutters; inside it was full of long passages and rooms with low ceilings." Stockingford, which lies about two miles from Nun-eaton, between that town and Arbury, is called Paddiford Common in the story. It was up Church Street that Mr. Tryan passed "through a pelting shower of nicknames and bad puns, with an *ad libitum* accompaniment of groans, howls, hisses, and hee-haws."

It is scarcely to be wondered at that, when the *incognito* of George Eliot was so carefully preserved—and yet the tales were so full of local incident and colour—an attempt should have been made to claim the authorship for another. This was the origin of the myth of Joseph Liggins, who was for some time supposed to be George Eliot. A table-rapper had spelt out the name of the great unknown as Liggers. Mr. Liggins of Nuneaton, a broken-down gentleman of very poor literary pretensions, did not reject the honour which was thrust upon him. He called himself George Eliot, and was more proud than ever after the appearance of "Adam Bede." A deputation of Dissenting parsons went out to see him, and found him washing his slop-basin at a pump. At a later period a subscription was got up for him, and George Eliot and Mr. Blackwood found it necessary to interfere. The myth was at last killed, though not without some difficulty, and there is little doubt that this absurd mistake delayed for some time the discovery of the true George Eliot.

George Eliot now abandoned these swallow flights for a more sustained effort, and began a novel which placed her at once in the first rank of authors, while it will always be regarded as a masterpiece of English literature. The manuscript of "Adam Bede," down to the end of chapter xiii., the second scene in the wood, was given to Mr. John Blackwood on February 28, 1858— the day on which he was introduced to the real George Eliot for the first time. He wished to examine the novel in order to see whether it would be advisable to print it in the Magazine, and in order to form a better judgment asked George Eliot to tell him the story, which for good reasons she declined to do. In April the Leweses started for Munich, chiefly for the purpose of seeing men of science, who might be useful to Lewes in

GEORGE ELIOT. 55

Strasse, for twenty florins a month, but did not begin
work for some little time. Among those who most
impressed them was the chemist Liebig, with whom they
dined, seeing "how men of European celebrity may put
up with greasy cooking in private life." At last, on May
15th, the eighteenth chapter of "Adam Bede" was
completed. George Eliot read it to Lewes, who was
much pleased. Eleven days later she had finished
chapter xx. On June 10th she writes in her diary,
"For the last week my work has been rather scanty
owing to bodily ailments. I am at the end of chapter
xxi., and am this morning going to begin chapter xxii.,"
the first of Book III. Three days later the entry runs,
"This morning at last free from headache and able to
write. I am entering on my history of the birthday
with some fear and trembling." The next month saw
the completion of the first five chapters of this book,
after which they started for Dresden—by way of Vienna.
The six weeks' stay at Dresden was one of the happiest
periods of George Eliot's life. It is difficult to see why
she did not more often create for herself a similar environment of circumstances. The day after their arrival
they secured their lodgings :—

"A whole apartment, of six rooms, all to ourselves, for 18s.
per week ! . . . By nine o'clock we were established in our new
home, where we were to enjoy six weeks' quiet work, undis-
turbed by visits and visitors. And so we did. We were as happy
as princes—are not—George writing at the far corner of the great
salon, I at my *Schrank* in my own private room, with closed doors.
Here I wrote the latter half of the second volume of 'Adam

Bede' in the long mornings that our early hours—rising at six o'clock
—secured for us. Three mornings in the week we went to the Picture
Gallery from twelve till one. . . . It was a charming life, our six weeks
at Dresden. There were the open-air concerts at the Grosser Garten
and the Brühlsche Terrasse, the Sommer Theater, where we saw our
favourite comic actor Merbitz; the walks into the open country,
and the grand stretch of sky all round; the Zouaves, with their
wondrous make-ups as women; Räder, the humorous comedian
at the Link'sche Bad Theater ; our quiet afternoons in our pleasant
salon—all helping to make an agreeable fringe to the quiet working
time."

To how many workers has Dresden been a similar
home of stimulus and repose !   Leaving it at the end
of August for Leipzig, they travelled from that town
night and day till they reached Richmond on September
2nd.   By this time Book IV. of " Adam Bede " was completed, all but the last chapter, which was finished at
Park Shot.   Her average rate of writing at Dresden
was a little more than eight hundred words a day.   The
chapter of "Amos Barton" describing Milly's death, which
we know was written at one sitting, is about double this
length.

The history of the composition of " Adam Bede," as
told by George Eliot, is too important to be omitted :—

" The germ of ' Adam Bede' was an anecdote told
me by my Methodist Aunt Samuel (the wife of my
father's younger brother),—an anecdote from her own
experience. We were sitting together one afternoon
during her visit to me at Griff, probably in 1839 or 1840,
when it occurred to her to tell me how she had visited
a condemned criminal—a very ignorant girl, who had

murdered her child and refused to confess; how she
had stayed with her praying through the night, and how
the poor creature at last broke out into tears, and con-
fessed her crime.   My aunt afterwards went with her in
the cart to the place of execution; and she described
to me the great respect with which this ministry of hers
was regarded by the official people about the gaol.   The
story, told by my aunt with great feeling, affected me
deeply, and I never lost the impression of that afternoon
and our talk together; but I believe I never mentioned
it, through all the intervening years, till something
prompted me to tell it to George in December, 1856,
when I had begun to write the 'Scenes of Clerical Life.'
He remarked that the scene in the prison would make a
fine element in a story, and I afterwards began to think
of blending this and some other recollections of my
aunt in one story, with some points in my father's early
life and character.   The problem of construction that
remained was to make the unhappy girl one of the chief
dramatis personæ, and connect her with the hero.   At
first I thought of making the story one of the series of
'Scenes,' but afterwards, when several motives had
induced me to close these with 'Janet's Repentance,'
I determined on making what we always called in our
conversation 'My Aunt's Story,' the subject of a long
novel, which I accordingly began to write on October 22,
1857.

   "The character of Dinah grew out of my recollections
of my aunt; but Dinah is not at all like my aunt, who
was a very small, black-eyed woman, and (as I was told,
for I never heard her preach) very vehement in her

style of preaching. She had left off preaching when I knew her, being probably sixty years old and in delicate health ; and she had become, as my father told me, much more gentle and subdued than she had been in the days of her active ministry and bodily strength, when she could not rest without exhorting and remonstrating in season and out of season. I was very fond of her, and enjoyed the few weeks of her stay with me greatly. She was loving and kind to me, and I could talk to her about my inward life, which was closely shut up from those usually round me. I saw her only twice again, for much shorter periods—once at her own home at Wirksworth in Derbyshire, and once at my father's last residence, Foleshill.

"The character of Adam, and one or two incidents connected with him, were suggested by my father's early life; but Adam is not my father any more than Dinah is my aunt. Indeed, there is not a single portrait in 'Adam Bede'; only the suggestions of experience wrought up into new combinations. When I began to write it, the only elements I had determined on, besides the character of Dinah, were the character of Adam, his relation to Arthur Donnithorne, and their mutual relations to Hetty,—*i.e.*, to the girl who commits child-murder,—the scene in the prison being, of course, the climax towards which I worked. Everything else grew out of the characters and their mutual relations. Dinah's ultimate relation to Adam was suggested by George, when I had read to him the first part of the first volume : he was so delighted with the presentation of Dinah, and so convinced that the reader's interest would centre in her, that he wanted her to be the principal figure at the last. I accepted the idea at once, and from the end of the third chapter worked with it constantly in view.

"The first volume was writtten at Richmond, and given to Blackwood in March [February 28th]. He expressed great admiration of its freshness and vividness, but seemed to hesitate about putting it in the Magazine, which was the form of publication he, as well as myself, had previously contemplated. He still *wished* to have it for the Magazine, but desired to know the course of the story. At *present* he saw nothing to prevent its reception in 'Maga,' but he would like to see more. I am uncertain whether his doubts rested solely on Hetty's relation to Arthur, or whether they were also directed towards the treatment of Methodism by the Church. I refused to give my story beforehand, on the ground that I would not have it judged apart from my *treatment*, which alone determines the moral quality of art; and ultimately I proposed that the notion of publication in 'Maga' should be given up, and that the novel should be published in three volumes at Christmas, if possible. He assented.

"I began the second volume in the second week of my stay at Munich, about the middle of April. While we were at Munich, George expressed his fear that Adam's part was too passive throughout the drama, and that it was important for him to be brought into more direct collision with Arthur. This doubt haunted me, and out of it grew the scene in the wood between Arthur and Adam; the fight came to me as a *necessity* one night at the Munich opera, when I was listening to 'William Tell' [May 30, 1858]. Work was slow and interrupted at Munich, and when I left I had only written to the beginning of the dance on the Birthday Feast; but at Dresden I wrote uninterruptedly and with great enjoyment in the long, quiet mornings, and there I nearly finished the second volume,—all, I think, but the last chapter, which I wrote here in the old room at Richmond, in the first week of September, and then sent the MS. off to Blackwood. The opening of the third volume—'Hetty's Journey'—was, I think, written more rapidly than the rest of the book, and was left without the slightest alteration of the first draft. Throughout the book I have altered little; and the only cases I think in which George suggested more than a verbal alteration when I read the MS. aloud to him, were the first scene at the Farm, and the scene in the wood between Arthur and Adam, both of which he recommended me to 'space out' a little, which I did.

"When, on October 29, I had written to the end of the love-scene at the Farm, between Adam and Dinah, I sent the MS. to Blackwood, since the remainder of the third volume could not affect the judgment passed on what had gone before. He wrote back in warm admiration, and offered me, on the part of the firm, £800 for four years' copyright [subsequently raised to £1,200]. I accepted the offer. The last words of the third volume were written and despatched on their way to Edinburgh, November the 16th, and now, on the last day of the same month, I have written this slight history of my book. I love it very much, and am deeply thankful to have written it, whatever the public may say to it—a result which is still in darkness, for I have at present had only four sheets of the proof. The book would have been published at Christmas, or rather early in December, but that Bulwer's 'What will he do with it?' was to be published by Blackwood at that time, and it was thought that this novel might interfere with mine."

"Adam Bede" was published at the beginning of February, 1859. The sensation caused by its appearance has seldom been equalled in literary history. It was felt that a new power had arisen in English letters. Darwin's ' Origin of Species" appeared in the same year, and the two books, so different in their characters, so similar in their originality, divided the attractions of the thinking world. Deeply as men's hearts were stirred by the story of Hetty, perhaps the strongest impression was excited by the racy language of Mrs. Poyser, as amusing as Sam. Weller in "Pickwick," and more true to life. A month after the book's appearance, Charles Buxton quoted in the House of Commons the words: " It wants to be hatched over again and hatched different." George Eliot tells us that all these sayings were her own, and were not a product of reminiscence. "I have no stock of proverbs in my memory; and there is not one thing put into Mrs. Poyser's mouth that is not fresh from my own mint." It is indeed extraordinary that a masterpiece of literature should have been produced at the first attempt by a woman nearly forty years of age. No doubt this revelation of her powers previously unknown to herself, which produced such momentous results, was caused by the union with Lewes—a marriage productive of the greatest happiness to both. The manuscript of " Adam Bede," written in exquisite handwriting on ruled paper, with scarcely an erasure, is dedicated to her husband in these words:—" To my dear husband, George Henry Lewes, I give the MS. of a work which would never have been written but for the happiness which his love conferred on my life." Similarly Lewes writes in his journal in January, 1859 :

" Walked along the Thames towards Kew to meet Herbert Spencer, who was to spend the day with us, and we chatted with him on matters personal and philosophical. . . . My acquaintance with him was the brightest ray in a very dreary, *wasted* period of my life. I had given up all ambition whatever, lived from hand to mouth, and thought the evil of each day sufficient. The stimulus of his intellect, especially during our long walks, roused my energy once more and revived my dormant love of science. His intense theorizing tendency was contagious, and it was only the stimulus of a *theory* which could have induced me to work. I owe Spencer another and a deeper debt. It was through him that I learned to know Marian—to know her was to love her,—and since then my life has been a new birth. To her I owe all my prosperity and all my happiness. God bless her ! "

George Eliot also writes on the last day of 1858 :

" The last day of the dear old year, which has been full of expected and unexpected happiness. ' Adam Bede ' has been written, and the second volume is in type. The first number of George's ' Physiology of Common Life,'—a work in which he has had much happy occupation—is published to-day ; and both his position as a scientific writer, and his inward satisfaction in that part of his studies, have been much heightened during the past year. Our double life is more and more blessed—more and more complete."

Although "Adam Bede" would never have been written without the stimulus of Lewes' sympathy, it may be doubted whether his specific influence in the composition of the book was advantageous. Mr. W. Call, a very competent critic, tells us in the *Westminster Review* that the violent conflict of Adam with Arthur is an offence to art, and that the commonplace marriage of Adam with Dinah is a disappointing close to the career of the sweet Methodist saint. He also complains that the reprieval episode is an artificial and mechanical contrivance. It would have been better if George Eliot had followed more closely the fate of the girl Voce who was condemned to death at the Nottingham Assizes and executed. At a later period she would have done this. Yet, as we have seen, these very features were inserted at the suggestion of Lewes, and would have been absent if George Eliot had maintained more confidence in her own insight and discrimination. "Adam Bede" has still the largest sale of any of George Eliot's works, although "Romola," perhaps, appeals more powerfully to a cultured few. Its power is due to the intensity with which it represents actual life. Here again it is probable that more was drawn from experience than she thought, as I have said. Robert Evans, like Adam Bede, was first a carpenter, then a forester, and then a land-agent. The friendship of Adam with Arthur was precisely that of Evans to young Newdigate, the Oldinport of "Amos Barton." We cannot tell how much of the relations sketched in the novel rested on facts. Hayslope is the lovely village of Ellastone in Staffordshire, which begins at the bridge over the Dove which separates it from Derbyshire. The village green is still to be seen there, and the Davenport or Donnithorne Arms, a public-house kept by an Evans, a young, handsome, and intelligent cousin of the novelist, serenely proud of the family to which he belongs. The willowed brook still runs at the bottom of the slope, but the old cottage of the Evans family has been changed into a larger residence. The recollection of Dinah's preaching still lingers in the place. One of her favourite sites for preaching was Roston Common, high land, now enclosed, on the Derbyshire side of the Dove above Norbury. A farm in the village was once held by a family named Poyser. Oakbourne is Ashbourne, Snowfield is Wirksworth, Eagledale is Dovedale, Norbourne is Norbury, Donnithorne Chase may be Calwich Abbey. The visitor to Norbury or Ellastone will find several carpenters' shops like Adam Bede's. The elder-tree which is described as growing at the door of the workshop is an early recollection, and George Eliot once told me, when we were standing in front of Cranbourne Tower looking over Windsor, how closely that tree was connected with the poetry of her life.

Most remarkable perhaps is the identification of Dinah Morris with Elizabeth Evans, the wife of Samuel, Adam's brother. She was born at Newbold, in Leicestershire, and, after spending a short time at Nottingham, settled at Wirksworth, in Derbyshire, where she worked in a tape-mill. She took early to preaching among the Wesleyans, being remarkable for her natural gifts, and for her deep spirituality. She joined the Methodists in 1797, and, to use her own words, determined to leave off all superfluities of dress; and while still a young girl she tramped from village to village all over the bleak treeless Derbyshire Hills, and into the fertile, undulating country of the adjoining county, gathering the poor around her, and speaking to them of the belief which suffused her own life. "I saw it my duty to be wholly devoted to God, and to be set apart for the Master's use." She lived in a rude, thatched, stone-built, four-roomed cottage, standing sideways to the road, with a bit of potato ground in front, just opposite the Harlaam tape-works which Samuel Evans managed, half a mile from the town of Wirksworth. In this cottage George Eliot stayed with her aunt. Although George Eliot disclaims the exact resemblance between Dinah Morris and Elizabeth Evans, advantage was taken of the celebrity given by the novel to erect a tablet in the Wesleyan Chapel, Chapel Lane, Wirksworth, to the memory of Mrs. Evans and her husband. The inscription runs thus—

"Erected by numerous friends to the memory of Elizabeth Evans, known to the world as 'Dinah Bede,' who during many years proclaimed alike in the open air, the sanctuary, and from house to house, the love of Christ. She died in the Lord May 9, 1849, aged 74 years. And of Samuel Evans her husband, who was also a faithful local preacher and class-leader in the Methodist Society. He finished his earthly course December 8, 1858, aged 81 years."

No sooner was "Adam Bede" completed than the "Mill on the Floss" was begun—another fragment

5

of real existence. George Eliot writes to Blackwood
on December 28th, " I have not yet made up my
mind what my next story is to be, but I must
not lie fallow any longer when the new year has
come." So on January 12, 1859, she went into town
with Lewes, and looked in the "Annual Register"
for cases of *inundations*, with an obvious view to the
catastrophe of the new novel. This was three days
before she had corrected the last proof-sheets of " Adam
Bede." Success had brought prosperity. After living
since her father's death in lodgings, she was now able to
take a house, Holly Lodge, Wandsworth, for seven years.
Thither they removed on February 5th, a deliciously
fresh bright day, the omen of a happy life to come.
Their first weeks were cheered by the success of " Adam
Bede." The journal tells us, under date March 26,
1859—

"George went into town to-day and brought me home a budget
of good news that compensated for the pain I felt in the coldness of
an old friend. Mr. Langford says that Mudie ' thinks he must have
another hundred or two of 'Adam'—has read the work himself,
and is delighted with it.' Charles Reade says it is ' the finest thing
since Shakespeare '—placed his finger on Lisbeth's account of her
coming home with her husband from their marriage—praises enthusiastically the style—the way in which the author handles the
Saxon language. Shirley Brooks also delighted. John Murray says
there has never been such a book. . . . Lucas delighted with
the book, and will review it in the *Times* the first opportunity."

At the same time George Eliot is able to write to Mr.
Blackwood—"About my new story, which will be a novel
as long as 'Adam Bede,' and a sort of companion
picture of provincial life, we must talk when I have the

pleasure of seeing you. It will be a work which will
require time and labour." A month later the old
diffidence comes over her—"Shall I ever write another
book as true as ' Adam Bede'? The weight of the
future presses on me, and makes itself felt even more
than the deep satisfaction of the past and present."

It was this feeling perhaps which made her turn to the
completion of "The Lifted Veil," which she finished on
April 29th, having begun it, she tells us, one morning at
Richmond, when her head was too stupid for more
important work. The story is interesting psychologically,
but not otherwise. It is apparently a sermon on the
text,

> " Prudens futuri temporis exitum
> Caliginosa nocte premit Deus."

The germ of the tale is found in the following passage,
which might be, and perhaps is, a quotation from a note-
book :—

" So absolute is our soul's need of something hidden and uncertain for the maintenance of that doubt and hope and effort which
are the breath of its life, that if the whole future were laid bare to us
beyond to-day the interest of all mankind would be bent on the
hours that lie between ; we should pant after the uncertainties of
our one morning and our one afternoon ; we should rush fiercely to
the Exchange for our last possibility of speculation, of success, of
disappointment ; we should have a glut of political prophets
foretelling a crisis or no crisis within the twenty-four hours left open
to prophecy. Conceive the condition of the human mind if all
propositions whatsoever were self-evident except one, which was to
become self-evident at the close of a summer's day, but in the
meantime might be the subject of question, of hypothesis, of debate.
Art and philosophy, literature and sciences, would fasten like bees
on that one proposition which had the merit of probability in it,

and be the more eager because their enjoyments would end with sunset.   Our impulses, our spiritual activities, no more adjust themselves to the idea of their future nullity, than the beating of our heart or the irritability of our muscles."

The story is uninteresting in itself, and the probabilities are not even decently preserved.   Why should a seer gifted with such prescience fail to foresee the two most important events in the story, that his brother was going to be killed, and that his wife was going to poison him? She writes in 1873 that she does not wish it reprinted at present.   "I care for the idea which it embodies, and which justifies its painfulness.   There are many things in it which I would willingly say over again, but I shall never put them in any other form."   The motto which expresses the central idea dates from the same year— 1873 :—

> "Give me no light, great heaven, but such as turns
> To energy of human fellowship :
> No powers save the growing heritage
> That makes completer manhood."

The rest of the year 1859 was taken up with writing " The Mill on the Floss," finished on March 21, 1860. It does not seem to have been a very happy year for George Eliot.   The house at Wandsworth, taken with such hopes of permanence, did not suit her; there was too much publicity with too many dusty lanes. Also the new novel made great demands upon her.   It was written more out of her own life than out of her reminiscences.   It must have been exhausting work to recall in all their fulness of detail those early days with her brother, now passed for ever, and it is probable that some of the more passionate scenes of the grown-up "Maggie" also made clutches at her heart-strings. Further the extraordinary success of "Adam Bede" seems to have saddened as well as gratified her. She was conscious of the weight of responsibility now resting upon her, and her congenital diffidence made her fear that she would never be able to write another book as good as her first. We find in her diary and letters no trace of the joyous work at Munich and Dresden. What a pity, we are constantly tempted to exclaim, that so much of her life was spent under depressing influences! "I am assured," she writes to Major Blackwood, "that 'Adam Bede' was worth writing—worth living through long years to write. But now it seems impossible to me that I shall ever write anything so good and true again. I have arrived at faith in the past, but not at faith in the future." The one happiness she gained at Wandsworth was her friendship with Mrs. Congreve. Otherwise, she writes to her, "I want to get out of this house —cut cables and drift about. I dislike Wandsworth." And again, "This place certainly becomes drearier to me as the summer advances. The dusty roads are all longer, and the shade is further off." There is a curious entry under the date of June 20, 1859—"We went to the Crystal Palace to hear the 'Messiah,' and dined afterwards with the Brays and Sara Hennell. I told them that I was the author of 'Adam Bede' and 'Clerical Scenes,' and they seemed overwhelmed with surprise. This experience has enlightened me a good deal as to the ignorance in which we all live of each

other." It is indeed very strange that these most
intimate friends should not have discovered the authorship
as Madame Bodichon was able to do ; and that they
should have been surprised that Marian Evans had produced the book.   There is rather a patronizing tone
about some of their letters, as if they regarded George
Eliot as necessarily an intellectual dependant, which
she naturally enough resented.   A hurried visit to
Lucerne in July was rather fatiguing than refreshing.
Bad spirits still weighed upon her.   " When ' Maggie '
is done," she writes to Blackwood, " and I have a
month or two of leisure, I should like to transfer
our present house, into which we were driven by
haste and economy, to some one who likes houses
full of eyes all round him.   I long for a house with some
shade and grass close round it—I don't care how rough
—and the sight of Swiss houses has heightened my
longing."   And a few days later she says to Mrs. Bray—

"The weight of my future life,—the self-questioning whether my
nature will be able to meet the heavy demands upon it, both of
personal duty and intellectual production,—bears upon me almost
continually in a way that prevents me even from tasting the quiet
joy I might have had in the *work done.*   Buoyancy and exaltation,
I fancy, are out of the question when one has lived so long as I
have . . . I feel no regret that the fame, as such, brings no pleasure;
but it *is* a grief to me that I do not constantly feel strong in
thankfulness that my past life has vindicated its uses, and given me
reason for gladness that such an unpromising woman-child was
born into the world."

Meanwhile the work goes on.   "Our great difficulty is
time," she writes to Miss Hennell.   "I am little better

than a sick nigger with the lash behind him at present."
A remark of hers to Madame Bodichon throws a
curious light on the difference between her earlier and
her later novels, between "Adam Bede" and "The
Mill on the Floss" on the one hand, and "Middlemarch" and "Daniel Deronda" on the other. "I do
wish much to see more of human life—how can one see
enough in the short years one has to stay in the world?
But I meant [referring to something which she had
written to her correspondent] that at present my mind
works with the most freedom and the keenest sense
of poetry in my remotest past, and there are many
strata to be worked through before I can begin to use,
artistically, any material I may gather in the present."
Her art did strive towards the acquisition of this
material, and eventually she accomplished its assimi-
lation.

The first instalment of "Maggie" sent to Blackwood
pleased him, and George Eliot writes, on August 17th—

"I am glad that my story cleaves to you. At present I have no
hope that it will affect people as strongly as 'Adam' has done.
The characters are on a lower level generally, and the environment less romantic. But my stories grow in me like plants, and
this is only in the leaf-bud. I have faith that the flower will
come."

Still we find her, in the middle of September, after a
short holiday at Weymouth, "in much anxiety and
doubt" about the new novel. The result of this was a
three days' visit to Gainsborough, the prototype of St.
Ogg's, which gave her some new ideas, and put her in
better hope. She was always apparently writing with

a view to the final catastrophe of the inundation. On October 16th she is able to write in her journal, " Have finished the first volume of my new novel, ' Sister Maggie '; have got my legal question answered satis- factorily; and, when my headache has cleared off, must go at it full speed." More interesting is the sketch given of herself at this period to M. Albert Durade, her host in Geneva, to whom she had not written for a very long period :

" In the last three years a great change has come over my life. . . . Under the influences of the intense happiness I have enjoyed from thorough moral and intellectual sympathy, I have at last found out my true vocation, after which my nature had always been feeling and striving uneasily without finding it. What do you think that vocation is? I pause for you to guess. I have turned out to be an artist—not as you are, with pencil and the palette, but with words. I have written a novel which people say has interested them deeply, and *not* a *few* people, but almost all reading England. It was published in February last, and already 14,000 copies have been sold. The title is ' Adam Bede,' and ' George Eliot,' the name on the title-page, is my *nom de plume*. I had previously written another work of fiction called ' Scenes of Clerical Life,' which had a great *literary* success, but not a great *popular* success, such as ' Adam Bede ' has had. . . . I think you will believe that I do not write you word of this out of any small vanity. My books are deeply serious things to me, and come out of all the painful discip- line, all the most hardly-learned lessons, of my past life. I write you word of it, because I believe that both your kind heart and Madame D'Albert's too will be touched with real joy, that one whom you knew when she was not very happy, and when her life seemed to serve no purpose of much worth, has been at last blessed with the sense that she has done something worth living and suffering for. . . . I am very much changed from the ' Minie ' of old days : the years have altered me as much inwardly as out- wardly. In some things, however, I am just the same—in some of

my failings, I fear ; but it is not a failing to retain a vivid remem-
brance of past scenes, and to feel warmly towards friends whose
kindness lies far back in the distance, and in these things I am the
same as when I used to walk on La Treille with you or Madame
D'Albert."

The scene between Mr. Tulliver and Wakem, in
Book III. chap. vii., was written on November 24, 1859.
The second volume was finished on January 16, 1860.
By this time it had been settled that the novel should be
called "The Mill on the Floss," at Blackwood's suggestion—in spite of the obvious rejoinder that the mill was
not on the Floss, but on a small tributary of it. "Sister
Maggie" would have been a far better title. Yet even
now she writes—

"I have been invalided for the last week, and, of course, am
a prisoner in the castle of Giant Despair, who growls in my ear
that 'The Mill on the Floss is detestable, and that the last
volume will be the climax of that general detestableness. Such is
the elation attendant on what a self-elected lady correspondent of
mine from Scotland calls my 'exciting career' !"

The last eleven pages of "The Mill on the Floss"
were written in a *furor* on the morning of March 21st.
Blackwood had previously consented to very liberal
terms—£2,000 for 4,000 copies of the three-volume
edition, £150 for 1,000 at 12s., and £60 for 1,000 at
6s.   Sixteen thousand copies of "Adam Bede" were
sold in the first year, and at this rate George Eliot would
have received £8,000 as her share.

There is no need to dwell on the extent to which the
early chapters of "The Mill on the Floss" are a picture
of the early life of George Eliot and her brother Isaac.

In this respect it resembles the " David Copperfield " of
Dickens. It is more to the purpose to quote her own
defence of the book in answer to the criticism of Sir
Edward Lytton :

"I return Sir Edward's critical letter, which I have read with
much interest. On two points I recognize the justice of his
criticism. First, that Maggie is made to appear too passive in the
scene of quarrel in the Red Deeps. If my book were still in MS.
I should—now that the defect is suggested to me—alter, or rather
expand, that scene. Secondly, that the tragedy is not adequately
prepared. This is a defect which I felt even while writing the
third volume, and have felt ever since the MS. left me. The
Epische Breite into which I was beguiled by love of my subject in
the two first volumes, caused a want of proportionate fulness in the
treatment of the third, which I shall always regret. The other
chief point of criticism—Maggie's position towards Stephen—is too
vital a part of my whole conception and purpose for me to be con-
verted to the condemnation of it. If I am wrong there—if I did
not really know what my heroine would feel and do under the
circumstances in which I deliberately placed her—I ought not to
have written this book at all, but quite a different book, if any. If
the ethics of art do not admit the truthful presentation of a
character essentially noble, but liable to great error—error that is
anguish to its own nobleness—then, it seems to me, the ethics of
art are too narrow, and must be widened to correspond with a
widening psychology."

Immediately after the completion of "The Mill on
the Floss," Mr. and Mrs. Lewes started for a tour in
Italy, to visit new scenes and gather new experiences.
This journey forms a dividing epoch in George Eliot's
artistic life, nearly as important as that of the journey
to Italy in the life of Goethe.

CHAPTER III.

THE journey to Italy occupied the second quarter of 1860. George Eliot has left us an account of her travels, which does not, however, contain anything particularly original. Rome appears to have pleased her little, Venice more, Florence most. The most important result of the expedition was the novel of "Romola," which arose directly out of her visit to Florence. George Eliot was not unlike other geniuses in setting a greater value on what others could do than on what she could accomplish easily herself, and in holding somewhat cheaply those talents which were most completely part of her nature. Although she recognized the fact that it was her vocation in life to write novels, she was wont to lament that this work was so much more liberally rewarded than the science of her husband, or the historical researches of other friends. Her mind also had a strong tendency towards erudition. The first literary task she planned was a table of ecclesiastical history. She continued to amass knowledge throughout her life. She revelled in Monteil's "History of France," a book which is neither a history nor a romance, but something between the two—an attempt to reconstruct the life of the Middle Ages as the Gallus and Charicles of Bekker that of ancient Rome. This tendency induced her to transplant modern psychological problems into the atmosphere of mediæval Florence—to produce a book which is a marvel of literary skill, which fascinates many minds, but does not represent moral struggles as forcibly as they would appear amongst familiar surroundings; which gives a picture of Italian life, marvellous indeed as an intellectual effort, but unreal to those who know Italy as well as she knew England. The composition of the book was a terrible strain. It made most serious demands upon her physical strength. It remains perhaps, the best of all historical novels, but a warning that no more should ever be attempted.

Lewes once told me that "Romola" grew out of a projected article on Savonarola, probably a review of his life by Signor Villari. This is hardly consistent with the account given in her letters. She writes to Major Blackwood, on May 27th, "There has been a crescendo of enjoyment in our travels; for Florence, from its relation to the history of Modern Art, has roused a keener interest in us even than Greece, and has stimulated me to entertain rather an ambitious project, which I mean to be a secret from every one but you and Mr. John Blackwood." Again she writes to Mr. Blackwood from Berne, on June 23rd, "I don't think I can venture to tell you what my great project is by letter, for I am anxious to keep it a secret. It will require a great deal of study and labour, and I am athirst to begin." On August 28th the secret is told:—

"When we were in Florence, I was rather fired with the idea of writing a historical romance—scene, Florence; period, the close of the fifteenth century, which was marked by Savonarola's career and martyrdom. Mr. Lewes has encouraged me to persevere in the project, saying that I should probably do something in historical romance rather different in character from what has been done before. But I want first to write another English story, and the plan I should like to carry out is this : to publish my next English novel when my Italian one is advanced enough for us to begin its publication a few months afterwards in ' Maga.' It would appear without a name in the Magazine, and be subsequently reprinted with the name of George Eliot. I need not tell you the wherefore of this plan. You know well enough the received phrases with which a writer is greeted when he does something else than what was expected of him. But just now I am quite without confidence in my future doings, and almost repent of having formed conceptions which will go on lashing me now until I have at least tried to fulfil them."

At Michaelmas, 1860, Mr. and Mrs. Lewes left Wandsworth, and came to a furnished house, 10 Harewood Square, which they took for six months. Here the idea of "Silas Marner" occurred to her, and delayed for a time the composition of "Romola." She describes herself as suffering from physical weakness and mental depression; as bitterly regretting the loss of the country, as being unable to execute work, and despairing of ever working well again. Still "Silas Marner " proceeded slowly, and only sixty-two pages were written in two months. On December 17th, they removed to 16 Blandford Square, and remained there for nearly three years. They hoped by the end of that time to have so far done their duty by their children as to be free to live where they desired. She announced her story to Blackwood in the following words :—

"I am writing a story which came *across* my other plans by a sudden inspiration. I don't know at present whether it will resolve itself into a book short enough for me to complete before Easter, or whether it will expand beyond that possibility. It seems to me that nobody will take any interest in it but myself, for it is extremely unlike the popular stories going; but Mr. Lewes declares that I am wrong, and says it is as good as anything I have done."

It is a story of old-fashioned village life, which had unfolded itself from the merest millet-seed of thought. By February 1st, page 209 had been reached, amidst great bodily discomfort; and a fortnight later, 230 pages of manuscript were sent to Blackwood. Amidst this work there are constant complaints about her health. She feels "old and ricketty," her " *malaise* is chiefly owing to the depressing influence of town air and town scenes." Why, we ask again, did she not move to more congenial surroundings? Was Mr. Lewes so uncompromising a Londoner? Mr. Blackwood found "Silas Marner" rather sombre. George Eliot replies to him—

" I hope you will not find it at all a sad story as a whole, since it sets—or is intended to set—in a strong light the remedial influences of pure, natural, human relations. The Nemesis is a very mild one. I have felt all through as if the story would have lent itself best to metrical rather than to prose fiction, especially in all that relates to the pyschology of Silas ; except that, under that treatment, there could not be an equal play of humour. It came to me first of all quite suddenly, as a sort of legendary tale, suggested by my recollection of having once, in early childhood, seen a linen-weaver with a bag on his back; but as my mind dwelt on the subject I became inclined to a more realistic treatment."

The last pages of the manuscript were sent off to Edinburgh on March 10, 1861.

"Silas Marner" is, perhaps, the novel of George Eliot which has earned the highest praise from literary craftsmen. It contains all her merits in high perfection, concentrated by the narrow limits in which the work is enclosed. The hero is one of those ordinary unexciting characters which she loved to choose. His joy over the hoarded guineas is something like that of David Faux, but the story of their loss and recovery has a far higher purpose than that depicted in Brother Jacob. Godfrey Cass is a reminiscence of Arthur Donnithorne and a foretaste of Tito, one of those weak, self-indulgent characters who are led by the impulse of the moment, and whose softness is a source of ruin to themselves and others. Mr. Macey is a kind of male Mrs. Poyser, full of witty sayings, hot from George Eliot's mint. "There's allays two 'pinions; there's the 'pinion a man has of himsen, and there's the 'pinion other folks have on him. There'd be two 'pinions about a cracked bell if the bell could hear itself." "I don't heed how the women are made. They wear nayther coat nor breeches; you can't make much out of their shapes." "He isn't come to his right colour yet: he's partly like a black-baked pie." These and many other gems sparkle in Macey's conversation. Dolly Winthrop is a reflection of Mrs. Poyser, and nothing is more graphic or more entertaining than her views on religious subjects. "I've looked for help in the right quarter, and give myself up to them as we must all give ourselves up to at the last; and if we've done our part it isn't to be believed as them as are above us 'ull be worse nor we are, and come short o' theirn.' "It comes into my head as them above has got a deal

tenderer heart nor what I've got—for I can't be anyways
better nor them as made me ; and if anything looks hard
to me, it's because there's things I don't know on ; and
for the matter o' that there may be plenty o' things I don't
know on, for it's little as I know—that it is." "All as
we've got to do is to trusten, Master Marner—to do the
right thing as far as we know, and to trusten. For if we
as knows so little can see a bit o' good and right, we may
be sure as there's a good and a right bigger nor what we
can know. I feel it i' my own inside as it must be so."
The sweeping away of the little chapel in which the first
injury was done to Silas is a fine image of the disappear-
ance of wrong done in the gristle of early life in the
larger and more liberal growth of later years. "Silas
Marner" draws but little on the author's personal recollections. No scene familiar in early life is described, no
friend of early years is portrayed. The experience from
which the characters are drawn is part of her life-blood,
but in other respects the tale is a pure product of imagination. The success of the book was considerable, and
the author appears to have been surprised at it.

"Silas Marner" ended, "Romola" was resumed, but
a long preparation was necessary for its production. The
first duty was a visit to Florence, which was reached at
the beginning of May. She saw that city mainly under
the guidance of Mr. Thomas Adolphus Trollope, who
was then engaged in writing his history of the Tuscan
capital. She remained there only thirty-four days, and Mr.
Trollope told me a few years afterwards how extraordinary it was that she should have gained so intimate a
knowledge in so short a space of time. However, her

bad spirits did not altogether desert her. He told me that one day, taking him aside into a retired street, she assured him that she considered it a great evil and wrong that she had ever been born. Some of her letters speak of her occupations :

" We have been industriously foraging in old streets and old books. I feel very brave just now, and enjoy the thought of work— but don't set your mind on my doing just what I have dreamed. It may turn out that I can't work freely and fully enough in the medium I have chosen, and in that case I must give it up : for I will never write anything to which my whole heart, mind, and con-science don't consent, so that I may feel that it was something—how-ever small—which wanted to be done in this world, and that I am just the organ for that little bit of work. . . . Mr. Lewes is kept in con-tinual distraction by having to attend to my wants—going with me to the Magliabecchian Library, and poking about everywhere on my behalf—I having very little self-help about me of the pushing and inquiring kind."

In her journal she reflects thus upon her visit : " Will it be all in vain ? Our morning hours were spent in look-ing at streets, buildings, and pictures, in hunting up old books, at shops or stalls, or in reading at the Maglia-becchian Library. Alas ! I could have done much more if I had been well ; but that regret applies to most years of my life."

The journal notes that "Romola" was begun on October 7, 1861. This, indeed, was not the real beginning of the novel as it stands at present, which dates from January 1, 1862. But before this time is reached much had to be gone through. On July 12th she tells Miss Hennell that she is fresh from six quarto volumes on the history of the monastic orders, and she had just begun a less

formidable modern book on the same subject, Montalem-
bert's "Monks of the West." Further, that she has been
reading the Survey of the Middle Ages contained in
the fifth volume of the "Philosophie Positive." "Few
chapters can be fuller of luminous ideas." On July 30th
she writes: "Read little this morning—my mind dwelling with much depression on the probability or improba-
bility of my achieving the work I wish to do. I struck
out two or three thoughts towards an English novel. I
am much affected with hopelessness and melancholy just
now, and yet I feel the value of my blessings." The
following extracts illustrate the painful efforts by which
"Romola" was brought to birth—

"*Aug.* 1. Struggling constantly with depression. . . . *Aug.* 10.
Walked with G. We talked of my Italian novel. . . . *Aug.* 12. Got
into a state of such wretchedness in attempting to concentrate my
thoughts on the construction of my story, that I became desperate,
and suddenly burst my bonds, saying, I will not think of writing ! . . .
Aug. 20. This morning I conceived the plot of my novel with new
distinctness. *Aug.* 24. These have been placid, ineffective days—
my mind being clouded and depressed."

Eleven days were spent at Malvern, during which Mrs.
Jameson's "Legends of the Monastic Orders" was
read, and the "Storia di San Marco," by Marchese,
begun. The journal continues :

"*Sept.* 23. I have been unwell ever since we returned from
Malvern, and have been disturbed from various causes in my work,
so that I have done scarcely anything except correct my own books
for a new edition. To-day I am much better, and hope to begin a more
effective life to-morrow. . . . *Oct.* 4. My mind still worried about my
plot—and without any confidence in my ability to do what I want.
Oct. 28 and 30. Not very well. Utterly desponding about my

book. *Oct.* 31. Still with an incapable head—trying to write, trying to construct, and unable. *Nov.* 6. So utterly dejected that, in walking with G. in the park, I had almost resolved to give up my Italian novel. *Nov.* 10. New sense of things to be done in my novel, and more brightness in my thoughts. Yesterday I was occupied with ideas about my next English novel ; but this morning the Italian scenes returned upon me with fresh attraction."

At last the cloud lifts. On December 8th, she relates to Lewes the conception of the story, with which he expressed great delight. "Shall I ever be able to carry out my ideas. Flashes of hope are succeeded by long intervals of dim distrust." On December 12th she finished writing the plot, and on January 1st she began the novel in its present form.

We learn from these extracts—which appear to me extremely valuable for the intellectual history of George Eliot—that the idea of "Romola" had been present to her mind for eighteen months before a word of the novel was written. No wonder that so deep a root was destined to support a tree so stately. "Romola" was eventually published in the *Cornhill Magazine*, and it is interesting to note that it was conceived, and begun, without any reference to the periodical in which it appeared, or to the publisher who should bring it into the world. On January 23, 1862, Mr. George Smith called in Blandford Square, and asked if George Eliot were open to a "magnificent offer." What this was does not precisely appear in Mr. Cross's book. On February 27th Mr. Smith offered to give £10,000 for the appearance of the novel in the *Cornhill*, and the entire copyright at home and abroad. The diary mentions, on May 23rd, that the sum given was £7,000, in twelve monthly payments. I have certainly heard on good authority that the sum eventually paid was £12,000, with the right of publication for four years. It was thus some time before "Romola" could be included in the regular series of George Eliot's works. The first part was published in the *Cornhill* for July, at which time three parts only had been completed. There is no doubt that the anxiety of publishing in numbers, and the necessity of producing a certain amount of copy at stated intervals, increased the strain, already too great, of creating a narrative in an artificial and unfamiliar medium. It was indeed a noble enterprize for the conductors of the *Cornhill* to purchase at so large a price the work of the first novelist of the day, and to have it illustrated by Frederick Leighton. But there is also no doubt that, heartily as "Romola" was welcomed, even in its inception, by competent judges, it for a time injuriously affected the circulation of the magazine. As the author warmed to her work the complaints of depression became less frequent. The summer was spent at Littlehampton, and by the end of October she had again contrived to be three parts in advance. At the end of November she is able to write to Mr. Durade: " In this world of struggles and endurance, we seem to have more than our share of happiness and prosperity, and I think this year's end finds me enjoying existence more than ever I did before, in spite of the loss of youth. Study is a keener delight to me than ever, and I think the affections, instead of being dulled by age, have acquired a stronger activity." However, as she neared the end of her task, the pressure became more severe. She writes on May 6th: "We have just returned from Dorking, whither I went a fortnight ago to have solitude. . . . The weather was severely cold for several days of my stay, and I was often ailing. That has been the way with me for a month and more, and in consequence I am backward with my July number of 'Romola,' the last part but one." To this Mr. Cross adds: "I remember my wife telling me, at Witley, how cruelly she had suffered at Dorking from working under a leaden weight at this time. The writing of 'Romola' ploughed into her more than any of her other books. She told me she could put her finger on it as marking a well-defined transition in her life. In her own words, 'I began it a young woman,—I finished it an old woman.'" Part xiii. was eventually completed and Tito killed, on May 16th, in great excitement. The final stroke to the novel was eventually put on June 9th. The manuscript, exquisitely written, with scarcely an erasure, after the date of the commencement and completion, bears this inscription: "To the Husband whose perfect love has been the best source of her insight and strength, this manuscript is given by his devoted wife, the writer."

It is a peculiarity of "Romola," as distinguished from other historical novels, that the object is, not so much to present a living picture of a particular period in history, as to create an historical background for characters whose interest lies in their intense moral significance. Romola, Tito, Tessa, Bardo, have all of them their homologues in other novels of George Eliot, but undoubtedly the form they take is affected and determined by the epoch in which they live. No doubt the particular portion of history in which the story is laid, the transition from the mediæval to the modern world, is especially worthy of accurate description; and with George Eliot's historical knowledge no fault is to be found. At the same time, it may be gravely doubted whether she ever really assimilated the essence of Italian life. In reading " Romola," with all its exquisite art, one regrets that the types which are drawn with such strength are not placed in an environment which the author can describe without effort. Hence some of those who are best acquainted with Italian life have never been able to concur in the laudation of " Romola." Such admirable judges as Robert Browning and William Story find a difficulty in reading it, from the falsity of life which it represents; and Miss Blind tells us that Mazzini and Rossetti were of the same opinion. To the last the Florentine contemporaries of Frà Girolamo seemed nineteenth-century men and women dressed up in the costume of the fifteenth. They thought that the book was not " native." Still the intensity of passion in the actors, the beauty of the language, and the charm of Florentine scenery which forms the background, induce many to rank it as the first of her masterpieces. Her own view of some aspects of the book is given in a letter to Mr. R. H. Hutton :—

"After reading your article on ' Romola ' with careful reference to the questions you put to me in your letter, I can answer sincerely that I find nothing fanciful in your interpretation. On the contrary, I am confirmed in the sameaction I felt when I first listened to the article, at finding that certain chief elements of my intention have impressed themselves so strongly on your mind, notwithstanding the imperfect degree in which I have been able to give form to my ideas. Of course, if I had been called on to expound my own book, there are other things that I should want to say, or things that I should say somewhat otherwise ; but I can point to nothing in your exposition of which my consciousness tells me that it is erroneous, in the sense of saying something which I neither thought nor felt. You have seized, with a fulness which I had hardly hoped that my book would suggest, what it was my effort to express in the presentation of Bardo and Baldassarre ; and also the relation of the Florentine political life to the development of Tito's nature. Perhaps even a judge so discerning as yourself could not infer from the imperfect result how strict a self-control and selection were exercised in the presentation of details. I believe there is scarcely a phrase, an incident, an allusion, that did not gather its value to me from its supposed subservience to my main artistic objects. But it is likely enough that my mental constitution would always render the issue of my labour something excessive—wanting due proportion. It is the habit of my imagination to strive after as full a vision of the medium in which a character moves as of the character itself. The psychological causes which prompted me to give such details of Florentine life and history as I have given, are precisely the same as those which determined me in giving the details of English village life in ' Silas Marner,' or the ' Dodson ' life out of which were developed the destinies of poor Tom and Maggie. But you have correctly pointed out the reason why my tendency to excess in this effort after artistic vision makes the impression of a fault in ' Romola' much more perceptible than in my previous books. And I am not surprised at your dissatisfaction with Romola herself. I can well believe that the many difficulties belonging to the treatment of such a character have not been overcome, and that I have failed to bring out my conception with adequate fulness. I am sorry she has attracted you so little ; for the great problem of her life, which essentially coincides with a chief problem in Savona rola's, is one that readers need helping to understand. But with regard to that and to my whole book, my predominant feeling is— not that I have achieved anything, but—that great facts have struggled to find a voice through me, and have only been able to speak brokenly. That consciousness makes me cherish the more

any proof that my work has been seen to have some true significance by minds prepared, not simply by instruction, but by that
religious and moral sympathy with the historical life of man, which
is the larger half of culture."

A remarkable feature in Romola's character should not
pass without notice, because it corresponds to something
which George Eliot probably found in her own nature.
It is the suddenness with which her passionate love turns
to loathing when she discovers that Tito has been false to
her. A woman with more tenderness might have urged
him to confession and repentance, and prevented him
from falling into his worst crimes. Romola's love is
based, not on passion alone, but on a deep admiration
for the moral qualities of the object loved. When the
roots of that admiration are withered, the love has
nothing more to feed upon, and dies.

The completion of "Romola" was followed by a long
rest of more than a year. It is not till September 6,
1864, that we find the entry in the journal, "I am reading about Spain, and trying a drama on a subject that
has fascinated me—have written the prologue, and am
beginning the First Act. But I have little hope of making
anything satisfactory." Such was the first commencement of "The Spanish Gypsy." In the meantime Mr. and
Mrs. Lewes had moved into the house which they occupied
until George Eliot's marriage with Mr. Cross—the house
most closely associated with her, with the composition of
"Felix Holt," "Middlemarch," and "Daniel Deronda,"
and with the gathering of that circle of friends which gave
her the opportunity of exercising a strong personal influence, and of becoming acquainted with that large sphere

of society and thought, the knowledge of which was
indispensable to her deepening views of art.   Few
houses in London have been the scene of stronger
and more interesting emotions.   The visitor on Sunday
afternoon rang at the gate, entered the porch of the
house, turned along the passage to the left, passing
by the dining-room and Mr. Lewes's study, and
entered the drawing-room by the door at the end
of the passage.   It was a double drawing-room without folding doors, decorated by Owen Jones, and
hung with Leighton's drawings for the illustration
of "Romola."   A bow window, with casements down
to the ground, looked on to the garden.   Mrs. Lewes
generally sat in an armchair at the left of the fireplace.
Lewes generally stood or moved about in the back
drawing-room, at the end of which was the grand piano,
on which, as far as I am aware, she never played during
these receptions.   In the early days of my acquaintance
the company was small, containing more men than women.
Herbert Spencer and Professor Beesly were constant visitors.   The guests closed round the fire and the conversation was general.   At a later period the company
increased, and those who wished to converse with the
great authoress whom they had come to visit took their
seat in turns at the chair by her side.   She always gave
us of her best.   Her conversation was deeply sympathetic, but grave and solemn, illumined by happy
phrases and by thrilling tenderness, but not by humour.
Although her features were heavy, and not well-propor-
tioned, all was forgotten when that majestic head bent
slowly down, and the eyes were lit up with a penetrating

and lively gaze. She appeared much greater than her books. Her ability seemed to shrink beside her moral grandeur. She was not only the cleverest, but the best woman you had met. You never dared to speak to her of her works ; her personality was so much more impressive than its product. At a later time the string of visitors became fatiguing to those who remembered the old days. The drawing-room was enlarged to hold them; and three fashionably dressed ladies, sweeping in, occupied the sofa, and seemed to fill the room. These Sunday afternoon receptions were a great strain upon her strength. When the last visitor had departed she would, if the weather were fine, seek refreshment in a brisk walk to dispel her headache, and to call back the circulation into her feet, the icy coldness of which was one of her perpetual trials. Her own study was a large room on the first floor. In front of her writing-table stood the cast of the Melian Asclepius — a present, I think, from Mr. Deutsch.

I remember Lewes telling me that George Eliot was to appear before the world as a poet. He said that her poetry had, above all other poetry that he knew, the most direct and immediate connection between the language and the sense. At the same time it may be doubted whether she ever wrote what can strictly be called poetry. She used verse as a vehicle for the concise and epigrammatic expression of thoughts which might have been clothed in prose ; but she lacked the passionate fire without which no poet can excel, and the gift of melodious language which should always adequately clothe expression and sometimes supplement its defects. The two first acts of " The Spanish Gypsy " were written in September and October, 1864, but the remaining five acts gave great difficulty in construction. The third act was, however, finished by Christmas Day. It then appears to have proceeded slowly, and the entry for February 21, 1865, runs, "Ill and very miserable. George has taken my drama away from me." By March 29th "Felix Holt" was begun, and was published in June, 1866. "The Spanish Gypsy" did not appear till two years later. Just at this time Lewes became editor of the *Fortnightly Review*, a new periodical based on the lines of the *Revue des Deux Mondes*, whose most important characteristic was to be the signing of the articles and the individual responsibility of the authors. It is strange to see how this movement, which began by a high-minded protest against anonymous journalism, has degenerated into a struggle for notorious names, and resulted in the conversion of magazines into menageries of social and literary lions.

My own friendship with George Eliot and her husband began through the *Fortnightly Review*. In the autumn of 1865 I was asked to review Mr. Adolphus Trollope's "History of Florence." I wrote the article in the Christmas vacation, and it was published early in the ensuing year. George Eliot was pleased to express approval of it. This led to a personal introduction, and to a friendship which lasted till her death.

"Felix Holt" was finished on May 31, 1866, having taken fourteen months to write. Although during that time George Eliot suffered from bad health, there is not as much information in her journal and letters about its composition as we find with regard to her other books. It is the weakest of her novels. Scarcely an incident in it appears to have grown out of her own life and experience, and there are few characters or situations which can have made any serious demand on her emotions. Perhaps the central idea of it was the renunciation of Esther, the giving up of a brilliant fortune and marriage for a humble lot with the man she loved and admired, a course of action which George Eliot often described in her writings and did not fail to inculcate in private life. "A supreme love, a motive that gives a sublime rhythm to a woman's life, and exalts habit into partnership with the soul's highest needs, is not to be had where and how she wills : to know that high initiation she must often tread where it is hard to tread and feel the chill air, and walk through darkness. It is not true that love makes all things easy : it makes us choose what is difficult." The greatest pains were spent upon the elaboration of the plot : and this was worked out with complicated legal technicalities, in which she had the assistance of Mr. Frederic Harrison. At first she appears to have consulted him on some legal questions, and writes in answer—

"The ample and clear statement you have sent me with kind promptness has put me in high spirits — as high spirits as can belong to an unhopeful author. Your hypothetical case of a settlement suits my needs surprisingly well. I shall be thankful to let Sugden alone, and throw myself entirely on your goodness, especially as what I wish is simply a basis of legal possibilities, and not any command of details. I want to be sure that my chords will not offend a critic accomplished in thorough-bass—not at all to present an exercise in thorough-bass."

After an interview the MS. of the first volume was sent to Mr. Harrison, and he was asked to pronounce on political as well as moral questions. She writes at the end of January, " I have received both your precious letters—the second edition of the case, and the subsequent note. The story is sufficiently in the track of ordinary probability; and the careful trouble you have so generously given to it has enabled me to feel a satisfaction in my plot which beforehand I had sighed for as unattainable."

Nearly three years elapsed between the completion of "Felix Holt" and the commencement of "Middlemarch." The only work of importance published by George Eliot in this interval was "The Spanish Gypsy," although it saw the birth of some of her other poems. Her literary life may be thus shortly summarized. After long preparation, first by translations and then by articles, her first efforts of imagination and construction were shown in the "Scenes of Clerical Life." Then follow the pair of English novels drawn chiefly from her own experience, "Adam Bede " and the "Mill on the Floss;" both novels of which "Amos Barton " gave a foretaste. "Silas Marner " and "Felix Holt " may be classed together as pure efforts of imagination. Each started with a central idea, which was worked out in the one case with success, in the other with failure. "Romola " was an attempt to combine erudition with imagination, to draw a picture of those moral struggles which detained her with so fascinating a spell, amid the surroundings of mediæval Italy. Although opinions are divided with regard to its artistic and dramatic merits, yet it will always remain one of those books which are indispensable for introducing the English mind to the appreciation and love of Italian scenes. "The Spanish Gypsy" is a companion work, dealing with Spain as "Romola" deals with Italy. After this George Eliot paused. She apparently recognized that her real strength lay in the English novel, but she needed new experience and material to feed her imagination. Her own reminiscences were exhausted. The attempt to construct a novel apart from experience had failed. She determined therefore to go more into the world which her literary reputation now opened up to her, to learn something more of men and their manners, to penetrate into the springs of the complex life which was passing around her, to prepare herself to write a romance of the modern world in which she lived, as true as the delineation of the society into which she had been born. This newly assimilated material was the foundation of "Middlemarch" and "Deronda,"—the first, in the opinion of the best judges, her masterpiece; the second, an attempt to solve deeper problems than she had before attempted, and to convert art to higher uses, perhaps a partial failure, but one more excellent and memorable than many successes.

The completion of "Felix Holt" was followed by a fortnight's holiday in Belgium and Holland. No sooner had George Eliot returned than she resumed her labours on "The Spanish Gypsy." The journal for August 30,

1866, tells us: "I have taken up the idea of my drama, "The Spanish Gypsy," again, and am reading on Spanish subjects—Bouterwek, Sismondi, Depping, Llorente, &c." About the same period she wrote more fully to Mr. Frederic Harrison:

> "At present I am going to take up a work again which I laid down before writing ' Felix.' It is—*but please, let this be a secret between ourselves*—an attempt at a drama, which I put aside at Mr. Lewes's request, after writing four acts, precisely because it was in that stage of creation—or *Werden*—in which the idea of the characters predominates over the incarnation. Now I read it again, I find it impossible to abandon it: the conceptions move me deeply, and they have never been wrought out before. There is not a thought or a symbol that I do not long to use: but the whole requires recasting; and, as I never recast anything before, I think of the issue very doubtfully. When one has to work out the dramatic action for one's self, under the inspiration of an idea, instead of having a grand myth or an Italian novel ready to one's hand, one feels anything but omnipotent. Not that I should have done any better if I had had the myth or the novel, for I am not a good user of opportunities. I think I have the right *locus* and historic conditions, but much else is wanting."

"The Spanish Gypsy" was begun in its new form on October 15, 1866. In the beginning of the following year George Eliot and her husband undertook a journey to Spain, similar to the visit to Florence which had been a preparation for "Romola." The crown of their journey was Granada. From that place she writes to Frederic Harrison and Mr. Blackwood:

> "I wish I could believe that you were all having anything like the clear skies and warm sun which have cheered our journeying for the last month. At Alicante we walked among the palm-

trees, with their golden fruit hanging in rich clusters, and felt a more delightful warmth than that of an English summer. Last night we walked out and saw the towers of the Alhambra, the wide Vega, and the snowy mountains by the brilliant moonlight. . . . Just now we read nothing but Spanish novels—and not much of those."

"We are both heartily rejoiced that we came to Spain. It was a great longing of mine, for, three years ago, I began to interest myself in Spanish history and literature, and have had a work lying by me, partly written, the subject of which is connected with Spain. Whether I shall ever bring it to maturity so as to satisfy myself sufficiently to print it, is a question not settled; but it is a work very near my heart. . . . Here, at Granada, the sun shines uninterruptedly; and in the middle of the day, to stand in the sunshine against a wall, reminds me of my sensations at Florence in the beginning of June."

The journal announces her return on March 16th. "I go to my poem and the construction of two works—if possible;"—undoubtedly "Middlemarch" and "Deronda." A little later she tells Mr. Blackwood:

"The work connected with Spain is not a romance. It is —prepare your fortitude—it is—a poem. I conceived the plot, and wrote nearly the whole as a drama in 1864. Mr. Lewes advised me to put it by for a time, and take it up again with a view to recasting it. He thinks hopefully of it. I need not tell you that I am *not* hopeful—but I am quite sure that the subject is fine. It is not historic, but has merely historic connections. The plot was wrought out entirely as an incorporation of my own ideas."

In the summer of this year the travellers, fresh from their return, came to see me at Eton College, where I was then residing. I shall never forget the visit, but I regret that it finds no mention in her diary, as it would be interesting to know her impressions of Eton and Windsor. They walked down with me to the playing fields in the morning, where a cricket match was in progress. Both dined at table with the boys in my house, and had an opportunity of seeing how Harold Transome looked when he was an Eton boy. In the afternoon they drove with me into Windsor Park, and enjoyed to perfection that loveliest of all views of Windsor from the green sward in front of Cranbourne Tower, a prospect now made less lovely by the too exuberant growth of trees. In the evening we rowed up the river, and George Eliot talked to me of her Spanish journey, and compared Windsor with Granada. I have been told by those who knew her long that she was awkward in her early womanhood, and had not acquired that repose and dignity which characterized her later years. I remember on this visit seeing some traces of the old "Maggie," the recollection of which is very precious to me. August and September were spent in a holiday in North Germany, during which little work was done. At Ilmenau, she wrote Fedalma's soliloquy, after her scene with Silva, and the ensuing dialogue between her and Juan. From Ilmenau she wrote me a long letter, describing the place, and asking me to join them at Dresden, and, as she expressed it, with kindly exaggeration, "to make some railway-station or corner of a street ever-memorable to them." I received the letter at Pontresina, and it is a deep regret to me that I did not accept the invitation. I have also most unfortunately lost all the letters I received from her during those years. I wrote to her not unfrequently on matters of education and literature, and her opinions on these subjects would have been of permanent value.

7

On her return from Germany "The Spanish Gypsy" was seriously resumed. Three thousand lines were completed by November 9th—a third of the projected poem. She wished to have the completed portion in type, to see how it looked, but feared the secret oozing out :—

"I want to keep myself free from all inducements to premature publication—I mean, publication before I have given my work as much revision as I can hope to give it while my mind is still nursing it. Beyond this, delay would be useless. The theory of laying by poems for nine years may be a fine one, but it could not answer for me to apply it. I could no more live through one of my books a second time, than I can live through last year again. But I like to keep checks on myself, and not to create external temptations to do what I should think foolish in another."

"Felix Holt's Address to Working-men," which appeared in *Blackwood's Magazine* for January, 1868, was written in the last week of November, 1867. It was composed at Mr. Blackwood's earnest request, to which it would have been better if she had not acceded. She says of it herself that, "perhaps, by a good deal longer consideration and gradual shaping I might have put the ideas into a more concrete, easy form." I dined with them alone in the middle of December, just as I was starting for Rome. George Eliot sat at the head of the table and carved. The conversation was chiefly on reminiscences of travel; but I remember it was then she told me the difficulty she had in understanding the full meaning of a Greek sentence, and the ease with which it was comprehended by Mr. Lewes. She describes herself at this time as a bundle of unpleasant sensations, with a palpitating heart and awkward manners, and professes a large charity for people who detest her ; yet no one was ever the object of more enthusiastic worship on the part of her friends.

At the end of February, 1869, George and Mrs. Lewes paid a visit to Cambridge. They stayed at the Bull Hotel, but were the guests jointly of Mr. W. G. Clark, then tutor of Trinity College, and public orator, and myself. I travelled down with them in the train, the journey giving me the impression that railway-travelling was irksome to her. She reiterated, I remember, strong warnings against reading in the train, a mode of study in which I have spent many happy hours. We dined in the evening, a small party, in Mr. Clark's rooms. I sat next to her, and she talked to me solemnly about the duties of life, about the shallow immorality of believing that all things would turn out for the best, and the danger of fixing our attention too much on the life to come, as likely to distract us from doing our duty in this world. The next day she breakfasted with me in my rooms in college. I shall not readily forget her exquisite courtesy and tenderness to the ladies whom I had invited to meet her. This was the first of several visits to Cambridge, which always gave her great pleasure. At a later period she was on several occasions the guest of Dr. Jowett, at Oxford. I asked her once what struck her as the most salient difference between the society of the two universities, and she replied that at Cambridge they all seemed to speak well of each other, whereas at Oxford they all criticized each other.

At this time "The Spanish Gypsy" is approaching

completion, and there are several notices of her work in the diary and the letters.

"I am reading about savages and semi-savages, and think that our religious oracles would do well to study savage ideas by a method of comparison with their own. Also, I am studying that semi-savage poem, the Iliad.' How enviable it is to be a classic. When a verse in the 'Iliad' bears six different meanings, and nobody knows which is the right, a commentator finds this equivocalness in itself admirable !"

She told me at a later period she always read some of the "Iliad" before beginning her work, in order to take out of her mouth the taste of the modern world. She writes to Mr. Blackwood that she chose the title "The Spanish Gypsy" a long time ago, because it is a title in the fashion of the elder dramatists, with whom she has perhaps more cousinship than with recent poets. Also at a later time: "The poem will be less tragic than I threatened: Mr. Lewes has prevailed on me to return to my original conception and give up the additional development, which I determined on subsequently. The poem is rather shorter in consequence." This, I suppose, refers to an intention to make the catastrophe turn upon the death of Don Silva. The poem was finally completed on April 29, 1868.

Her own account of the origin and purpose of the "Spanish Gypsy" cannot be omitted from this biography :—

"The subject of 'The Spanish Gypsy' was originally suggested to me by a picture which hangs in the Scuola di San Rocco at Venice, over the door of the large Sala containing Tintoretto's frescoes. It is an Annunciation said to be by Titian. Of course I had seen numerous pictures of this subject before, and the subject had always attracted me. But in this my second visit to the Scuola di San Rocco, this small picture of Titian's, pointed out to me for the first time, brought a new train of thought. It occurred to me that here was a great dramatic motive of the same class as those used by the Greek dramatists, yet specifically differing from them. A young maiden, believing herself to be on the eve of the chief event of her life—marriage—about to share in the ordinary lot of womanhood, full of young hope, has suddenly announced to her that she is chosen to fulfil a great destiny, entailing a terribly different experience from that of ordinary womanhood. She is chosen, not by any momentary arbitrariness, but as a result of foregoing hereditary conditions : she obeys. ' Behold the handmaid of the Lord.' Here, I thought, is a subject grander than that of 'Iphigenia,' and it has never been used. I came home with this in my mind, meaning to give the motive a clothing in some suitable set of historical and local conditions. My reflections brought me nothing that would serve me except that moment in Spanish history when the struggle with the Moors was attaining its climax, and when there was the gypsy race present under such conditions as would enable me to get my heroine and the hereditary claim on her among the gypsies. I required the opposition of race to give the need for renouncing the expectation of marriage. I could not use the Jews or the Moors, because the facts of their history were too conspicuously opposed to the working out of my catastrophe. Meanwhile the subject had become more and more pregnant to me. I saw it might be taken as a symbol of the part which is played in the general human lot by hereditary conditions in the largest sense, and of the fact that what we call duty is entirely made up of such conditions; for even in cases of just antagonism to the narrow view of hereditary claims, the whole background of the particular struggle is made up of our inherited nature. Suppose for a moment that our conduct at great epochs was determined entirely by reflection, without the immediate intervention of feeling which supersedes reflection, our determination as to the right would consist in an adjustment of our individual needs to the dire necessities of our lot, partly as to our natural constitution, partly as sharers of life with our fellow-beings. Tragedy consists in the terrible difficulty of this adjustment.

> ' The dire strife
> Of poor Humanity's afflicted will,
> Struggling in vain with ruthless destiny.'

Looking at individual lots, I seemed to see in each the same story, wrought out with more or less of tragedy, and I determined the elements of my drama under the influence of these ideas.

" In order to judge properly of the dramatic structure, it must not be considered first in the light of a doctrinal symbolism, but in the light of a tragedy representing some grand collision in the human lot. And it must be judged accordingly. A good tragic subject must represent a possible, sufficiently probable,

not a common action ; and to be really tragic, it must
represent irreparable collision between the individual and
the general (in different degrees of generality). It is the
individual with whom we sympathize, and the general of
which we recognize the irresistible power. The truth
of this test will be seen by applying it to the greatest
tragedies. The collision of Greek tragedy is often that
between hereditary, entailed Nemesis, and the peculiar
individual lot, awakening our sympathy, of the particular
man or woman whom the Nemesis is shown to grasp
with terrific force. Sometimes, as in the ' Oresteia,' there
is the clashing of two irreconcilable requirements—two
duties, as we should say in these times. The murder
of the father must be avenged by the murder of the
mother, which must again be avenged. These two
tragic relations of the individual and general, and of two
irreconcilable ' oughts,' may be—will be—seen to be
almost always combined. The Greeks were not taking
an artificial, entirely erroneous standpoint in their art—
a standpoint which disappeared altogether with their
religion and their art. They had the same essential
elements of life presented to them as we have, and their
art symbolized these in grand schematic forms. The ' Pro-
metheus ' represents the ineffectual struggle to redeem
the small and miserable race of man, against the stronger
adverse ordinances that govern the frame of things with
a triumphant power. Coming to modern tragedies, what
is it that makes ' Othello ' a great tragic subject ? A
story simply of a jealous husband is elevated into a
most pathetic tragedy by the hereditary conditions of
Othello's lot, which give him a subjective ground for

distrust. Faust, Rigoletto ('Le Roi s'Amuse'), Brutus. It might be a reasonable ground of objection against the whole structure of ' The Spanish Gypsy ' if it were shown that the action is outrageously improbable, lying outside all that can be congruously conceived of human actions. It is *not* a reasonable ground of objection that they would have done better to act otherwise, any more than it is a reasonable objection against the ' Iphigenia ' that Agamemnon would have done better not to sacrifice his daughter.

" As renunciations coming under the same great class, take the renunciation of marriage, where marriage cannot take place without entailing misery on the children.

" A tragedy has not to expound why the individual must give way to the general : it has to show that it is compelled to give way, the tragedy consisting in the struggle involved, and often in the entirely calamitous issue in spite of a grand submission.   Silva presents the tragedy of entire rebellion : Fedalma, of a grand sub- mission, which is rendered vain by the effects of Silva's rebellion : Zarca, the struggle for a great end, rendered vain by the surrounding conditions of life.

" Now what is the fact about our individual lots ?   A woman, say, finds herself on the earth with an inherited organization : she may be lame, she may inherit a disease, or what is tantamount to a disease : she may be a negress, or have other marks of race repulsive in the community where she is born, &c., &c.   One may go on for a long while without reaching the limits of the commonest inherited misfortunes.   It is almost a mockery

to say to such human beings, ' Seek your own happiness.'
The utmost approach to well-being that can be made in
such a case is through large resignation and acceptance
of the inevitable, with as much effort to overcome any
disadvantage as good sense will show to be attended
with a likelihood of success. Any one may say, that is
the dictate of mere rational reflection. But calm can,
in hardly any human organism, be attained by natural
reflection. Happily, we are not left to that. Love, pity,
constituting sympathy, and generous joy with regard to
the lot of our fellow-men, come in—have been growing
since the beginning—enormously enhanced by wider
vision of results—by an imagination actively interested
in the lot of mankind generally ; and these feelings
become piety—*i.e.*, loving, willing submission, and heroic
Promethean efforts towards high possibilities which may
result from our individual life.

" There is really no moral ' sanction' but this inward
impulse. The will of God is the same thing as the will
of other men, compelling us to work and avoid what
they have seen to be harmful to social existence. Dis-
joined from any perceived good, the divine will is simply
so much as we have ascertained of the facts of existence
which compel obedience at our peril. Any other notion
comes from the supposition of arbitrary revelation.

" That favourite view, expressed so often in Clough's
poems, of doing duty, in blindness as to the result, is likely
to deepen the substitution of egoistic yearnings for really
moral impulses. We cannot be utterly blind to the
results of duty, since that cannot be duty which is not
already judged to be for human good. To say the

contrary, is to say that mankind have reached no inductions as to what is for their good or evil.

" The art which leaves the soul in despair is laming to the soul, and is denounced by the healthy sentiment of an active community. The consolatory elements in ' The Spanish Gypsy ' are derived from two convictions or sentiments which so conspicuously pervade it that they may be said to be its very warp on which the whole action is woven. These are—(1) The importance of individual deeds; (2) The all-sufficiency of the soul's passions in determining sympathetic action.

" In Silva is presented the claim of fidelity to social pledges : in Fedalma the claim constituted by an hereditary lot less consciously shared.

"With regard to the supremacy of Love ; if it were a fact without exception that man or woman never did renounce the joys of love, there could never have sprung up a notion that such renunciation could present itself as a duty. If no parents had ever cared for their children, how could parental affection have been reckoned among the elements of life ? But what are the facts in relation to this matter ? Will any one say that faithfulness to the marriage tie has never been regarded as a duty, in spite of the presence of the profoundest passion experienced after marriage ? Is Guinevere's conduct the type of duty ? "

" The Spanish Gypsy " is a deeply impressive work. No one can read it without emotion. It is easy to understand that the author of it was reluctant to withhold it from the world. Its composition raises the question as to whether some things are better said in poetry than in prose. Had "The Spanish Gypsy" been a prose romance, we should have been tired with the perpetual strain of high-flown diction, and with the slight tinge of unreality in the characters. The rhetorical enthusiasm of Schiller's "Don Carlos," difficult to endure in poetry, would have been unbearable in prose. At the same time it is doubtful whether the "Spanish Gypsy" had not better have remained a tragedy in pure dramatic form. The mixture of description and dialogue is awkward, beautiful though the description may be. We also feel that the author's energies did not sustain her to the end. The first part (or act) is re-written and re-modelled to an extent which does not appear to be the case in the later portions. Also it can scarcely be called poetry. It may be doubted whether there is a line of it which has really taken its place among the household words of our language. The best passages are those which deal with psychological subtleties, the effect of the Angelus in the first part, and Fedalma's unconscious recognition of her father. Silva's description of his love :

> " The only better is a past that lives
> On through an added Present, stretching still
> In hope unchecked by shaming memories
> To life's last breath ; "

Zarca's account of his race, Fedalma's acknowledgment of the claim of filial duty—all these are more finely expressed than they could have been in prose. On the other hand, the lyrics are very disappointing. They halt and hobble. Their music, which ought to sigh or whisper, screeches, now and again, like the wheels of a

Portuguese wine-cart.   The only song with a lilt to it
is the first of Aria's, and even that is commonplace.
George Eliot had the gift of concentrated expression, but
not the gift of song.

The remainder of the year 1868 was spent in travel
and study.   Two months were given to a tour in
Germany and Switzerland.   A visit to Dr. Allbutt, at
Leeds, gave her a glimpse of hospital life which bore
fruit in "Middlemarch."   A journey to Derbyshire in
November renewed early recollections.   At the close of
the year she is able to hint that it has been as rich in
blessings as any year of their double life, and that
she enjoys a more even cheerfulness, and a continually
increasing power of dwelling on the good that is given
to her, and dismissing the thought of small evils.

CHAPTER IV.

ON January 1, 1869, George Eliot's diary announces: "I have set myself many tasks for the year—I wonder how many will be accomplished ?—a novel called 'Middlemarch,' a long poem on Timoleon, and several minor poems." It seems as if the work upon "The Spanish Gypsy" had opened up a vein of poetry in her, which, although it produced nothing of the same importance, has enriched our literature with much that it could not afford to lose. The somewhat slight poem of "Agatha," a recollection of St. Märgen near Freiburg—where, as George Eliot tells us, she had "the sensation of standing upon a round world"—and the turning into verse of Boccaccio's story "How Lisa loved the King," occupied the first six weeks of the year. Then followed a spring visit of nine weeks to Italy. Three days after her return, Thornton Lewes, a young man of twenty-five, arrived from Natal with an incurable spine disease, and George Eliot lavished upon him all the affectionate care of a mother. Her notices of this trial are very touching: "Our poor Thornie came back to us about seventeen days ago. We can never rejoice enough that we were already at home, seeing that we held it impossible for him to set out on his voyage until at least six weeks later than he did. Since he arrived, our lives have been chiefly absorbed by cares for him ; and though we now have a nurse to attend on him constantly, we spend several hours of the day by his side. There is joy in the midst of our trouble, from the tenderness towards the sufferer being altogether unchecked by anything unlovable in him." He lingered till October 19th, when the diary tells us : "This evening at half-past six our dear Thornie died. He went quite peacefully. For three days he was not more than fitfully and imperfectly conscious of things around him. He went to Natal on the 17th October 1863, and came back to us on the 8th May, 1869. Through the six months of his illness, his frank impulsive mind disclosed no traces of evil feeling. He was a sweet-natured boy—still a boy, though he had lived for twenty-five years and a half. On 9th August, he had an attack of paraplegia, and although he partially recovered from it, it made a marked change in him. After that he lost a great deal of his vivacity, but he suffered less pain. This death seems to me the beginning of our own."

In the meantime "Middlemarch" had been slowly progressing. An introduction was written on July 19th. Characters were meditated on July 23rd, and on August 2nd the novel was actually begun, but not in the form in which we now have it. The part first composed was probably a portion of Book I. chapter xi. On Sept. 1st George Eliot notes that she meditated characters and conditions for "Middlemarch"; and three weeks later she asks Mr. Congreve to get her some information about provincial hospitals, which is necessary to her imagining the conditions of her "hero." This shows that in her first conception Lydgate was to have been the central character of the book. During this interval the "Brother and Sister" Sonnets, which contain so many reminiscences of George Eliot's early life, were written, and the "Legend of Jubal" was begun. After their son's funeral the parents retired into the country for the remainder of the year: so that 1869 marks a comparatively unproductive period in George's Eliot's mental history. "Jubal" was completed on January 13, 1870, and March and April were occupied with a journey to Berlin and Vienna. "Jubal" is the deepest and most eloquent of her poems. Although it has the defect of all her verse, except, perhaps, the Positivist hymn, "O may I join the choir invisible," the absence of that thrilling power of diction which ought to be the main characteristic of poetry, yet it is impossible to remain unmoved by the deep problems of life and work with which the poem deals, and the eloquence and intensity with which the theme is treated. Her next production was "Armgart," in some respects a pendant to "Jubal," suggested, probably, by one of the Harrogate concerts. The year 1870 passed away, as its predecessor had done, without the production of much literary fruit.

However we find that George Eliot notes at the end of the year: "I have written only one hundred pages—good printed pages—of a story which I began about the opening of November, and at present mean to call 'Miss Brooke.' Poetry halts just now." There is also a previous entry in the diary for December 2nd: "I am experimenting in a story ('Miss Brooke') which I began without any very serious intention of carrying it out lengthily. It is a subject which has been recorded among my possible themes ever since I began to write fiction, but will probably take new shapes in the development." These hundred pages would bring the story down to the engagement of Casaubon to Dorothea. We thus see that "Middlemarch," as we now have it, is the fusion of two independent stories, one concerned with the marriage of an elderly pedant to a young wife, and the other with the struggles of a young doctor in a country town. It is possible that "Miss Brooke" may contain the story which George Eliot intended to have included in the "Scenes of Clerical Life," and which she speaks of as the "clerical tutor." It is also significant that the writing of this tale was preceded by a visit to the Rector of Lincoln College at Oxford, where she saw a good deal of University society, and would have had an opportunity of studying both learning and pedantry in their various phases.

On March 19, 1871, George Eliot writes, "I have written 236 pages (print) of my novel, which I want to get off my hands by next November. My present fear is that I have too much matter—too many *momenti.*" It appears that by this time the fusion of the two plots had been determined upon, but the final elaboration of the work had not yet become a purpose. The plan, however, must have been formulated by July, at the close of which she wrote to Mr. Blackwood :

"I don't see how I can leave anything out, because I hope there is nothing that will be seen to be irrelevant to my design, which is to show the gradual action of ordinary causes rather than exceptional, and to show this in some directions which have not been from time immemorial the beaten path—the Cremorne walks and shows of fiction. But the best intentions are good for nothing until execution has justified them. And you know I am always compassed about with fears. I am in danger in all my designs of parodying dear Goldsmith's satire on Burke, and think of refining when novel readers only think of skipping."

In September she announced to M. Durade that she is preparing "a long, long book." "Middlemarch" was published in eight monthly parts, each being printed as a neat and compact volume in the usual novel type, very different to the parts in which the novels of Dickens and Thackeray first saw the light. The first part was published on December 1, 1871, under the title of "Miss Brooke." It was at once received as a masterpiece, although in her letters she continually expresses misgivings that people should rate it as highly as they do. Perhaps she was conscious that it had not been conceived in her mind as a whole. The book also is stronger from representing rather the intertwining and conflicting currents of actual life than attempting to emphasize a particular purpose of instruction. No doubt the effect of the book was intensified by its appearance in instalments, and by the fact that the interest excited by it was similar to that aroused by the gradual development of human action and affairs. The labour was at an end in September, 1872, making a period of three years and nine months between the conception of the novel and its final execution. An interesting account is given of it in a letter to Mr. Alexander Main:

"I have finished my book ('Middlemarch'), and am thoroughly
8

at peace about it—not because I am convinced of its perfection, but because I have lived to give out what it was in me to give, and have not been hindered by illness or death from making my work a whole, such as it is. When a subject has begun to grow in me, I suffer terribly until it has wrought itself out—become a complete organism ; and then it seems to take wing and go away from me. *That* thing is not to be done again,—that life has been lived. I could not rest with a number of unfinished works on my mind. When they—or rather when a conception has begun to shape itself in written words— I feel that it must go on to the end before I can be happy about it. Then I move away and look at it from a distance without any agi. tations.''

Miss Blind, in the chapter on " Middlemarch " in her " Life of George Eliot," devotes much space to describing the life of the authoress and her husband at Shottermill in Hampshire, where part of the story was written. It was the custom for husband and wife during these later years to spend the autumn months in some retired country spot devoted entirely to work and study. I was more than once employed by them to discover such a place for their summer haunts, but I was never successful in suiting all their requirements. Their address was kept secret even from their most intimate friends, and anything which might interfere with the absolute regularity of their lives was carefully avoided, and although, as a special privilege, I was more than once invited to visit them in their different solitudes, I could never bring myself to take advantage of the permission.

A very large sum (£12,000, it is believed) was paid for "Middlemarch," but considering that nearly twenty thousand copies at two guineas had been sold by the close of 1874, the amount paid does not appear excessive.

The completion of " Middlemarch " was followed as usual
by a journey to the Continent ; this time to Homburg, by
way of Trèves.   Homburg was at that time the home of
gaming-tables, and George Eliot witnessed a scene which
inspired the opening of " Daniel Deronda."   She writes
in two letters—

" The air, the waters, the plantations here, are all perfect—' only
man is vile.'   I am not fond of denouncing my fellow-sinners, but
gambling being a vice I have no mind to, it stirs my disgust even more
than my pity.   The sight of the dull faces bending round the gaming-
tables, the raking up of the money, and the flinging of the coins
towards the winners by the hard-faced croupiers, the hateful, hideous
women staring at the board like stupid monomaniacs—all this seems
to me the most abject presentation of mortals grasping after something called a good, that can be seen on the face of this little earth.
. . Hell is the only right name for such places."

And again what is evidently a presentation of Gwendolen Harleth :

" The saddest thing to be witnessed is the play of a young lady,
who is only twenty-six years old, and is completely in the grasp of
this mean, money-making demon.   It made me cry to see her young
fresh face among the hags and brutally stupid men around her."

In May, 1873, an interesting visit was paid to Cambridge, which probably had also a serious influence on
the fortunes of " Deronda."   It was the occasion of that
momentous conversation with Mr. Frederick Myers, in
the roundabout at Trinity, which is thus recorded in his
essays :—

" I remember how, at Cambridge, I walked with her once in the
Fellows' Garden of Trinity, on an evening of rainy May ; and she,
stirred somewhat beyond her wont, and taking as her text the three

words which have been used so often as the inspiring trumpet call
of men—the words God, Immortality, Duty—pronounced with
terrible earnestness how inconceivable was the first, how un-
believable the second, and yet how peremptory and absolute the
third. Never, perhaps, have sterner accents affirmed the sovereignty
of impersonal and unrecompensing Law. I listened, and night fell,
her grave, majestic countenance turned towards me like a sibyl's in
the gloom ; it was as though she withdrew from my grasp, one by
one, the two scrolls of promise, and left me the third scroll only,
awful with inevitable fates. And when we stood at length and
parted, amid that columnar circuit of the forest-trees, beneath the
last twilight of starless skies, I seemed to be gazing, like Titus at
Jerusalem, on vacant seats and empty halls—on a sanctuary with no
Presence to hallow it, and heaven left lonely of a God."

To use her own words, "We were invited ostensibly
to see the boat-race, but the real pleasure of the visit
consisted in talking with a hopeful group of Trinity
young men." She wrote to me enthusiastically of the
visit, and in speaking of one young man, who may have
been the prototype of Deronda, said that he was so
handsome that for some time she thought of nothing
else, but that she afterwards discovered that his mind
was as beautiful as his face.

Two months, again, in the summer of 1873, were spent
in foreign travel. This is referred to in the following
letter to Dr. Clifford Allbutt, which he has kindly
allowed me to publish—

"THE PRIORY, 21, NORTH BANK, REGENT'S PARK,
"*Nov.* 1, '73.
"DEAR DR. ALLBUTT,—Thanks for a very pleasant proof that
you bear us in your mind and heart. Your letter came just in time
to find us here, for we only yesterday returned from a house in the
country, to which we went at the beginning of September. Before

then, we had been for nine weeks in France and Germany, passed in the delightful region of the Vosges, which was new to us. I cannot say that our health has been particularly flourishing amidst all these enjoyments. Happiness, of which we seem to have more than any one we know, does not have the effect of making us fat and strong. I often laughingly compare ourselves to two mediæval saints painted by a very naïve master. Our bodies seem to shrink, like the *Peau de Chagrin*, with every year of happiness. Just now, however, Mr. Lewes, who has been for some time below his usual standard, is improving, and I have no unusual bodily grievance to complain of. Your ailments are more important, because you are younger and have more working time before you, and I don't like to read of your having worn yourself into an irritable state before you took your holiday. It is difficult to avoid such results, though, for a man whose energy goes out in mental work. Even where there is no external pressure the interest of the work is almost sure to get a wearing intensity. I think this was the cause of Mr. Lewes's flagging in the spring. For two years before he had been in a state of greater intellectual enjoyment than I had ever observed in him, the study of mathematics especially having made the world fresh to nim. His first (introductory) volume is soon to be out now, but he is calmly certain that very few will care about its discussions. No human being can be more happily constituted than he in relation to his work. He has quite an exceptional enjoyment in the doing, and has no irritable anxieties about it when done.

" As to the Johnsonian biography, he has had nothing to do with it, except the recommendation to Mr. Main to set about the work, and the writing of a brief preface.

". . . Your suggestions about lessening the inconveniences of writing could not come to a more appreciative person. I have for the last three years taken to writing on my knees, throwing myself backward in my chair, and having a high support to my feet. It is a great relief not to bend, and in this way at least I get advantage from the long-sightedness which involves the early need of glasses. Mr. Lewes is obliged to stoop close to his desk. But Dr. Liebreich condemns my arrangement as forcing up my knees too much, and he has devised a sort of semi-couch which seems to be perfection so far as the physical conditions of my writing are concerned. But how if

I have nothing else worth the writing ! It is in vain to get one's back and knees in the right attitude if one's mind is superannuated. Some time or other, if death does not come to silence one, there ought to be deliberate abstinence from writing—self-judgment which decides that one has no more to say. The public conscience about authorship wants quickening sadly—don't you think so? Happily for me, I have a critic at hand whom I can trust to tell me when I write what ought to be put behind the fire.

"Mr. Lewes unites with me in best regards to Mrs. Allbutt and yourself. We do not despair of being in your neighbourhood again some day, and taking a glimpse of you in your new home.

"Yours always warmly and sincerely,

"M. G. LEWES."

Another letter, written to Dr. Allbutt some years previously, possesses great interest—

"MY DEAR DR. ALLBUTT,—I had conjectured the fact, that some call of duty had summoned you back to Leeds earlier than you had expected.

"Since you refer to our conversation, I must tell you that I am always a little uneasy about my share in the talk when it has turned on religion.

"The weaknesses of one's mind are always taken by surprise in hasty discussion, and the chief result left in the consciousness is that of having misrepresented the dearest beliefs. My books are a form of utterance that dissatisfies me less, because they are deliberately, carefully constructed on a basis which even in my doubting mind is never shaken by a doubt, and they are not determined, as conversation inevitably is, by considerations of momentary expediency. The basis I mean is my conviction as to the relative goodness and nobleness of human dispositions and motives. And the inspiring principle which alone gives me courage to write is, that of so presenting our human life as to help my readers in getting a clearer conception and a more active admiration of those vital elements which bind men together and give a higher worthiness to their existence; and also to help them in gradually dissociating these elements from the more transient forms on which an outworn teaching tends to make them dependent. But, since you have read my books, you must perceive that the bent of my mind is conservative rather than destructive, and that denial has been wrung from me by hard experience—not adopted as a pleasant rebellion. Still, I see clearly that we ought, each of us, not to sit down and wail, but to be heroic and constructive, if possible, like the strong souls who lived before, as in other cases of religious decay.

"I dare not enter on these wide, wide subjects in a letter—for to write a letter at all, except about necessary details, is a difficult overcoming of indolence to me; but in relation to your despairing words that we seem to 'be reaching the limits of our scheme,' I wish you could thoroughly consider (if you have not already done so) whether it is probable that in a stage of society in which the ordinary standard of moral possibility, nay, of moral requirements, is still so low as I think you must recognize it to be, the highest possible religion has been evolved and accepted?

"If we were talking again, I should like to express what I fear was far from evident the other night—my yearning affection towards the great religions of the world which have reflected the struggles and needs of mankind, with a very different degree of completeness from the shifting compromise called 'philosophical theism.' But I am sure your favourite Marcus Aurelius would not have approved of my eagerness to say everything. I should try to make use of other interviews rather to get instructed by your rich practical experience —experience grievously wanting to me, whose life is passed chiefly in study and always in domestic ease. The invitation you give us is very tempting and pretty. If there came some beautiful autumnal weather, and other conditions were favourable in the third week of September, we might perhaps indulge ourselves with a journey into Yorkshire, get some breezes on the moors, and accept for a couple of days the pleasure your goodness offers us of seeing Leeds in your company. It is just the sort of thing I should like to do—to go over the Hospital with you.

"Mr. Lewes, I grieve to say, is headachy again—frequently suffering from a malaise, which is sadly at war with the ardent interest that prompts him to work. He unites with me in the desire to express sincere gratification that we have come to know you in spite of distance.

> " Believe me, yours always truly,
> " M. G. LEWES."

Little information about the composition of " Daniel Deronda ". is to be found in the published journals and letters of George Eliot. By the beginning of 1875 she had reached chapter xv. Part II., where Grandcourt and Deronda come into contact. But the usual distrust of herself beset her. " I am suffering much from doubt as to the worth of what I am doing, and fear lest I may not be able to complete it so as to make it a contribution to literature, and not a mere addition to the heap of books." In August she writes to Mr. Cross, " My book seems to me so unlikely ever to be finished in a way that will make it worth giving to the world, that it is a kind of glass in which I behold my infirmities." In the beginning of October she is able to inform Mr. Blackwood that half the book is completed, but she adds, " I can't say that I am at all satisfied with the book, or that I have a comfortable sense of doing in it what I want to do ; but Mr. Lewes *is* satisfied with it, and insists that since he is as anxious as possible for it to be fine, I ought to accept his impressions as trustworthy. So I resign myself." The new novel received the warm commendation of Mr. John Blackwood and his principal collaborators. He expressed some anxiety about the fate of Gwendolen, and is reassured by the author in the following terms: " It will, perhaps, be a little comfort to you to know that poor Gwen is spiritually saved, but ' so as by fire.' Don't you see the process already beginning? I have no doubt you do, for you are a wide-awake reader." On December 25th she is able to record in her diary that the two first volumes are in print, and that the first book is to be published on February 1st. She adds—

"I have thought very poorly of it myself throughout, but George and the Blackwoods are full of satisfaction in it. Each part as I see it before me *im Werden* seems less likely to be anything less than a failure; but I see on looking back this morning—Christmas Day —that I really was in worse health and suffered equal depression about 'Romola'; and, so far as I have recorded, the same thing seems to be true of 'Middlemarch.' I have finished the fifth book, but am not far on in the sixth, as I hoped to have been—the oppression under which I have been labouring having positively suspended my power of writing anything that I could feel satisfaction in."

By the middle of March, 1876, she is deep in the fourth volume, half of which was finished by the middle of April: the whole was completed in the first week of June. Her absorption in her work did not prevent her from giving much kind thought to the affairs of her friends. I have in my possession a precious letter of hers, dated March 2, 1875, which I cannot refrain from publishing. It may be of assistance to others who are in need of similar help and encouragement. I was then a master at Eton, but for many reasons the work was distasteful to me. I was anxious to transfer myself to the University, where I had promise of employment, but I was restrained by the reluctance to desert a cause which I believed to be important, and to which I had devoted many years of my life, and by the disinclination to break up my mother's comfortable home. In this difficulty I wrote to George Eliot, who had now for some years been to me a very dear and confidential friend, told her of my resolution to remain at Eton, and asked for her opinion.   Her reply was as follows—

"Your letter shall be sacred.   I am glad to know that you have made up your mind to endure and persevere—words easy to write as advice, but hard to follow out in the patient action of days, months, years.   Perhaps the most difficult heroism is that which consists in the daily conquests of our private demons, not in the slaying of world-notorious dragons.   Certainly it seems to me that the finest course of action you can pursue will be to impose the utmost restraint on impatience, and look at your life simply as the problem of carrying out your ideas of usefulness at Eton as far as may be without dangerous collisions.   To further this happiness and beneficence of your life—even apart from that question of your dear mother's feeling—you should have a precise conception of an alternative to your present task, an equivalent social contribution, before you unlink yourself.   But I gather that your resolution is thoroughly formed, and I rejoice.   We shall see you at the end of this fiercely menacing March.   You are young enough to dare travel at that time of year which we used to find everywhere cruel, south as well as north."

The part of " Deronda " about the success of which George Eliot felt most hesitation was that which referred to the Jews.   It is not clear when her interest in the Jews began.   Perhaps it arose from her friendship with Mr. Emmanuel Deutsch, who impressed her deeply. The treatment of the gypsies in " The Spanish Gypsy " shows her profound reverence for race and for inherited traditions.   Her generous sympathies would also be called out by the sense of unmerited persecution.   At any rate, she took the greatest pains to prepare herself for writing about this peculiar people.   The Jewish colour in " Deronda " is almost faultless ; it is certainly much more

free from errors than the picture of mediæval Italy presented in "Romola." George Eliot obtained access to
a large library of Jewish literature in London, and the
books preserved still show traces of her untiring labours.
By "Deronda," and by the protest against the "Juden-
hetze" contained in the essays of "Threophrastus Such,"
she has earned the undying gratitude of the best repre-
sentatives of the Jewish race throughout the world. An
interesting account of her own view of the situation is
given in a letter to Mrs. Harriet Beecher Stowe, written
in October, 1876—

"As to the Jewish element in 'Deronda,' I expected from first to
last, in writing it, that it would create much stronger resistance, and
even repulsion, than it has actually met with. But precisely because
I felt that the usual attitude of Christians towards Jews is—I hardly
know whether to say more impious or more stupid, when viewed in the
light of their professed principles, I therefore felt urged to treat
Jews with such sympathy and understanding as my nature and
knowledge could attain to. Moreover, not only towards the Jews,
but towards all Oriental peoples with whom we English come in
contact, a spirit of arrogance and contemptuous dictatorialness is
observable which has become a national disgrace to us. There is
nothing I should care more to do, if it were possible, than to rouse
the imagination of men and women to a vision of human claims in
those races of their fellow-men who most differ from them in customs
and beliefs. But towards the Hebrews we western people, who
have been reared in Christianity, have a peculiar debt, and, whether
we acknowledge it or not, a peculiar thoroughness of fellowship in
religious and moral sentiment. Can anything be more disgusting
than to hear people called 'educated' making small jokes about
eating ham, and showing themselves empty of any real knowledge
as to the relation of their own social and religious life to the history of
the people they think themselves witty in insulting? They hardly
know that Christ was a Jew. And I find men, educated, supposing
that Christ spoke Greek. To my feeling, this deadness to the

history which has prepared half our world for us, this inability to find interest in any form of life that is not clad in the same coat-tails and flounces as our own, lies very close to the worst kind of irreligion. The best that can be said of it is, that it is a sign of the intellectual narrowness—in plain English, the stupidity—which is still the average mark of our culture.

" Yes, I expected more aversion than I have found. But I was happily independent in material things, and felt no temptation to accommodate my writing to any standard except that of trying to do my best in what seemed to me most needful to be done ; and I sum up with the writer of the Book of Maccabees, 'If I have done well, and as befits the subject, it is what I desired ; and if I have done ill, it is what I could attain unto.'"

The completion of "Deronda" was followed by another spell of foreign travel, from which husband and wife returned much refreshed. They had intended to go to the Maritime Alps, but it was an exceptionally hot summer and they found the rest and refreshment they needed in the higher valleys of Eastern and Central Switzerland. The year ended happily. The journal records on December 1st :—

" Since we came home at the beginning of September, I have been made aware of much repugnance, or else indifference, towards the Jewish part of ' Deronda,' and of some hostile as well as adverse reviewing. On the other hand, there have been the strongest expres-sions of interest—some persons adhering to the opinion, started during the early numbers, that the book is my best. Delightful letters have here and there been sent to me ; and the sale, both in America and in England, has been an unmistakable guarantee that the public has been touched. Words of gratitude have come from Jews and Jewesses, and these are certain signs that I may have contributed my mite to a good result. The sale hitherto has ex-ceeded that of ' Middlemarch,' as to the £2 2s. four-volume form, but we do not expect an equal success for the guinea edition, which has lately been issued."

The close of this year was also marked by the purchase of a country house in Surrey: the Heights, Witley, near Godalming. It was in view of Blackdown, the home of Tennyson, and Hind Head. Mr. Cross says of it that it quite fulfilled all expectations as regards beauty and convenience of situation, but that he is not quite sure that it was bracing enough for health.

The entry in the journal dated November 10, 1877, records that the Leweses went thither, at the beginning of June, after a delightful visit to Cambridge. I remember the occasion well. George Eliot and her husband were the guests of Mr. Henry Sidgwick. I met them at dinner one day, and they lunched with me on another. The authoress was more tender, more dignified, and more impressive than ever, showing especial delight in the details of my new home and life. I remember the interest she showed in an American type-writing machine, which had recently been given to me, expressing at the same time, with some archness, the fear lest the type-writer should not only reveal its utterances in print, but should multiply them after the manner of a printing-press, thus adding to the number of worthless books. Mr. Edmund Gurney and his wife were of the party, and Mr. Fuller Maitland delighted George Eliot with music, especially in his performance of Beethoven's Lichnowski Sonata. A rather large party had been asked to meet them, and as most of the guests had never met George Lewes and his wife before, there was some excitement to hear the words which might fall from their lips. The silence was broken by Lewes saying to her, "Why, my dear, you surely don't like that heavy black Bavarian beer, do you?" an unexpected beginning of memorable table-talk.

The year closed with its accustomed retrospect .

"To-day [Dec. 31, 1877] I say a final farewell to this little book, which is the only record I have made of my personal life for sixteen years and more. I have often been helped, in looking back in it, to compare former with actual states of despondency from bad health or other apparent causes. In this way a past despondency has turned to present hopefulness. But of course, as the years advance, there is a new rational ground for the expectation that my life may become less fruitful. The difficulty is to decide how far resolution should set in the direction of activity, rather than in the acceptance of a more negative state. Many conceptions of work to be carried out present themselves, but confidence in my own fitness to complete them worthily is all the more wanting, because it is reasonable to argue that I must have already done my best. In fact, my mind is embarrassed by the number and wide variety of subjects that attract me, and the enlarging vista that each brings with it. I shall record no more in this book, because I am going to keep a more business-like diary. Here ends 1877."

A letter to Mrs. Bray, in June, 1878, gives an account of an interesting dinner at Mr. Goschen's, at which George Eliot met the Crown Prince and Princess of Germany.

"The Crown Prince is really a grand-looking man, whose name you would ask for with expectation, if you imagined him no royalty. He is like a grand antique bust—cordial and simple in manners withal, shaking hands, and insisting that I should let him know when we next came to Berlin, just as if he had been a Professor Gruppe, living *au troisième. She* is equally good-natured and unpretend-ing, liking best to talk of nursing soldiers, and of what her father's taste was in literature. She opened the talk by saying, ' You know my sister, Louise '—just as any other slightly embarrassed mortal might have done. We had a picked party to dinner—Dean of Westminster, Bishop of Peterborough, Lord and Lady Ripon, Dr. Lyon Playfair, Kinglake (you remember ' Eôthen '—the old gentleman is a good friend of mine), Froude, Mrs. Ponsonby (Lord Grey's grand-daughter), and two or three more ' illustrations; ' then a small detachment coming in after dinner. It was really an interesting occasion."

The summer of 1878 was spent at Witley, in the pre-paration of " Theophrastus Such." The health of both husband and wife was far from satisfactory. " We have had 'a bad time,' in point of health," she writes to Mr. John Blackwood, in September, 1878, " and it is only quite lately that we have both been feeling a little better. The fault is all in our own frames, not in our air or other circumstances; for we like our home and neighbourhood better and better. The general testimony and all other arguments are in favour of this district being thoroughly healthy. But we both look very haggard in the midst of our blessings."

It must indeed be impressed on the mind of any student of George Eliot's life, not only how much she was affected by climatic surroundings, but how little suited the air of England was to her constitution, and especially the air of London. She lived there possibly for the sake of her husband, who had spent all his life in London literary society, and who perhaps would have found it difficult to carry on his work under any other conditions. There is a touching notice of this in the last paragraph of " Looking Backward," in the " Impressions of Theophrastus Such."

" I cherish my childish loves—the memory of that warm little nest in which my affections were fledged. Since then I have learnt

to care for foreign countries, for literature foreign and ancient, for
the life of continental towns dozing round the cathedrals, for the
life of London, half sleepless with eager thought and strife, with
indigestion as with hunger ; and now my consciousness is chiefly of
the busy, anxious metropolitan sort. My system responds sensitively
to the London weather-signs, political, social, literary ; and my
bachelor's hearth is imbedded where by much craning of head and
neck I can catch sight of a sycamore in the Square yonder. I
belong to the ' Writers of London.' Why, there have been many
voluntary exiles in the world, and probably in the very first exodus
of the patriarchal Aryans—for I am determined not to fetch my
examples from races where talk is of uncles and no fathers—some
of those who sallied forth went for the sake of a loved companionship, when they would willingly have kept sight of the familiar
plains, and of the hills to which they had first lifted up their eyes."

It was shortly after this that I saw George Eliot for
the last time. In October, 1878, I was asked to meet
her, Mr. Lewes, and the Russian novelist, Turguenieff,
at the hospitable country house of Mr. Bullock Hall, at
Six-Mile Bottom, near Newmarket. The only others present were the late Mr. Munro, the editor of Lucretius, and
Mr. Sedley Taylor. They had driven in the afternoon
to see the races at Newmarket, and George Eliot was
full of admiration for the beautiful horses. Dogs were
her favourite animals, but she had plenty of affection to
spare for other species of our dumb companions. As
we all sat together in the closing twilight, she made
Turguenieff repeat to us, in his slow, broken English, what
he had already related to George Eliot in private, the
story of a play which he had seen in Paris, the reception
of which by a French audience threw, as he considered,
a strong and unfavourable light on the French character.
A woman in early life had married a scamp, who deserted

her, leaving two children, a son and a daughter. She
fled with them to the lake of Geneva, where she united
herself with a wealthy merchant with whom she lived
for twenty years, the children being brought up as his.
At last her husband discovered her retreat, came unexpectedly to the home, and revealed to the son that he
was his father. The merchant, afterwards entering,
saluted his supposed daughter with the customary kiss.
The son immediately struck him on the face and cried,
"You have not the right to do that," upon which the
audience applauded loudly, as if he had done an heroic
action. Turguenieff alone stood up in his box and
hissed. George Eliot hung eagerly upon his words as he
told the tale. Lewes sat at some distance. Such was
the French view of marriage, preferring the shadow to
the substance, the legal tie to the bond of custom,
affection, and gratitude. The party broke up deeply
stirred, and Lewes said that the English would have
behaved just as badly. It seemed to me strange that
George Eliot should insist on hearing for a second time
every detail of an imaginary story, which appeared to
touch so nearly the deepest problems of her own life.

At dinner Lewes proposed Turguenieff's health, in
an admirable speech, as the greatest living novelist.
Turguenieff replied, repudiating the compliment and
transferring it to George Eliot. In the drawing-room
Turguenieff told stories of Victor Hugo, of his arrogance
and his ignorance. Turguenieff had once asked Hugo who
was Galgacus, whom he had included in a list of orators in
some poem. "I have not an idea," replied Hugo; "but
it is a fine name." Turguenieff had talked to him of

9

Goethe. "Yes," said Hugo, "I admire Goethe ; I have read his 'Wallenstein.'" Upon Turguenieff remarking that "Wallenstein" was the work of Schiller and not of Goethe, Hugo said "I have never read a line of these gentlemen, but I know them as well as if I had written them myself." At another time Hugo said to Turguenieff, "As for me, I look upon Goethe as Jesus Christ would have looked upon Messalina." Mr. Munro was asked by Lewes to inscribe his name in a special album, and Lewes told me that, in his opinion, and in that of competent judges, his translation of Lucretius, apart from all other merits, was one of the finest pieces of English in the language. There was also some talk about Russian literature, and Turguenieff was asked to recite some Russian poetry, upon which he delivered to us a piece of Puschkin. I left next morning early, before the rest of the party had risen, certainly with no foreboding that within two months Lewes would be dead, and that I should never see George Eliot again.

Details of Lewes's last illness are given in two letters to Mr. John Blackwood, dated November 23rd, and November 25th. The first reads thus :

"When Mr. Lewes sent you my MS. the other morning, he was in that state of exhilarated activity which often comes with the sense of ease after an attack of illness which had been very painful. In the afternoon he imprudently drove out, and undertook, with his usual eagerness, to get through numerous details of business, over-fatigued himself, and took cold. The effect has been a sad amount of suffering from feverishness and headache, and I have been in deep anxiety— am still very unhappy, and only comforted by Sir James Paget's assurances that the actual trouble will be soon allayed."

Two days later she wrote :

" Mr. Lewes continues sadly ill, and I am absorbed in nursing him. When he wrote about Parliament meeting, he was thinking that it would be called together at the usual time—perhaps February. The book can be deferred without mischief. I wish to add a good deal, but of course I can finish nothing now until Mr. Lewes is better. The doctors pronounced him in every respect better yesterday, and he had a quiet night, but since five o'clock this morning he has had a recurrence of trouble. You can feel for him and me, having so lately known what severe illness is."

George Lewes died on November 28, 1878.

Although overwhelmed with grief, George Eliot set herself immediately to rear the most fitting monument to her husband's memory by preparing his papers for publication, and by founding a studentship to be called by his name. The following letter to Dr. Allbutt refers to this subject :

"THE PRIORY, 21, NORTH BANK, REGENT'S PARK,
" *Feb.* 20, '79.

" DEAR DR. ALLBUTT,—Your letter is among the most precious signs of sympathy that my kind friends have given me, because of what you say in it about my husband's influence over students. That is what he himself cared for as among the chief aims of life. I am tempted to ask you whether it would be otherwise than repugnant to you—whether you would have any satisfaction in writing, not a eulogistic, but a plain statement of your observation and experience in relation to the effect of my husband's work, to be printed in quotation, but not (unless you wished it) with your name, simply as a testimony of an experienced physician whose judgment is not simply that of a professional man, but of a scientific experimenter. I want, if I can, to write a ' *characteristik* ' of my loved one—no memoir, but a brief sketch of his mental and moral qualities, and his way of looking at the work he tried to do.

"Just now I am ill. Sir James Paget and Dr. Andrew Clark say I shall get better, but in the meantime my comparative incapacity for the work I want to do makes me anxious.

"Can you help me with any suggestions as to founding (now while I live) some Lectureships or other efficient instrument of teaching Biology (including Psychology) in memory of my husband, and to be called by his name? I am trying to get good advice, knowing how difficult it is to make an endowment a 'good custom' which shall not in the end become corrupt.

"Please give my best remembrances to your wife, who I hope is strong enough to enjoy the blessedness of your united life.

"Always yours gratefully,

"M. G. LEWES.

"I have not yet seen any one except our son Charles, and am unequal to anything more than feeble thinking and writing in relation to those chief objects. Any word you can send me will be valued."

Her own last work had to stand over for the present. She writes to Mr. Blackwood on February 25th:

"Pray do not announce 'Theophrastus' in any way. It would be intolerable to my feelings to have a book of my writing brought out for a long while to come. What I wish to do is to correct the sheets thoroughly, and then have them struck off and laid by till the time of publication comes. One reason which prompted me to set about the proofs—in addition to my scruples about occupying the type—was that I was feeling so ill, I thought there was no time to be lost in getting done everything which no one else would do if I left it undone. But I am getting better, I think ; and my doctors say there is nothing the matter with me to urge more haste than the common uncertainty of life urges on us all."

The proofs were soon corrected, and it was arranged that the book should be published with a notice that it had been placed in the publisher's hands in the previous November. On reading the revise she was so much

dissatisfied with the work that she thought of re-writing
it, but reflection on that "uncertainty of life" and strength
induced her to agree to its publication in May, with the
possibility of a second series, supposing that she lived
and kept her faculties.

"Theophrastus Such" has probably fewer readers
than any of George Eliot's works, but it is well worth
careful reading and remembering. It contains studies of
character, such as might form the rough drafts for future
novels, embodying moral lessons which she desired to
convey. The style is weighty and periodic, influenced
by the English of the seventeenth century which she
loved so well. The compact statement of arguments, the
subtlety of analysis and insight are as apparent as in any
of her works. The humour is sometimes admirable, at
others heavy and laboured ; there is little dramatic
interest. "Theophrastus" does not exist as a personality,
and the veil which divides him from the writer herself is
of varying degrees of density. Still the book furnishes
many "wise, witty, and tender sayings," and from its
inherent truthfulness and absence of affectation is a most
valuable source of information for the feelings and
opinions which lay deepest at her heart. "Looking
Backward" is full of autobiographical recollections ;
"the modern Hep, Hep, Hep," the cry with which the
Jews were persecuted, is a plain and solemn exposition
of the feelings which prompted the defence of the Jews
in "Deronda." The book shows no failure of intellectual
power, but is, perhaps, indicative of a lower degree of
physical energy, which prevented her from undertaking the
arduous task of constructing a new novel, and submitting

herself to pangs which her diary so pathetically recalls. George Eliot writes of it to Mr. Blackwood at the beginning of April :

"I enclose the proof of title-page and motto. Whether the motto (which is singularly apt and good) should be on the title-page or fly-leaf, I leave you to judge. Certainly everybody who does not read Latin will be offended by its claiming notice, and will consider that only the deepest-dyed pedantry could have found the motive for it. But I will not leave it out altogether."

There is little more to record of George Eliot's life. Her marriage with Mr. John Cross took place on May 6, 1880. It would be wrong to attempt to present any other account of this than that which Mr. Cross has himself given in the life of his wife. The marriage was severely criticized at the time by her best friends. This was due to various causes. Second marriages are absolutely forbidden by the Positivist creed, and her breach of this rule would be sure to alienate all who were of this persuasion. The world, which had forgiven her relations with Lewes, on the ground that they arose from an over-mastering devotion, was shocked when it found that the affection which had caused such an act of sacrifice was capable of being succeeded by another equally strong. The difference of nearly twenty years between the age of the bride and bridegroom also gave occasion for remark. On the other hand, no one can have studied the character of George Eliot, even superficially, without being convinced how necessary it was for her to have some one to depend upon, and how much her nature yearned for sympathy and support. No better companion could certainly have been found than Mr. Cross, with his strong vigorous sense, manly character, and business habits. Some crisis seems to have occurred on April 22, 1879, when Mr. Cross tells us that he received the following note : "I am in dreadful need of your counsel. Pray come to me when you can—morning, afternoon, or evening." From that time he saw George Eliot constantly. They read Dante and undertook many studies together. Under these influences her health and spirits seemed to improve. Madame Bodichon writes of her on June 5th :

" I spent an hour with Marian. She was more delightful than I can say, and left me in good spirits for her—though she is wretchedly thin, and looks in her long, loose, black dress like the black shadow of herself. She said she had so much to do that she must keep well —'the world was so *intensely interesting*.' She said she would come *next year* to see me. We both agreed in the great love we had for life. In fact, I think she will do more for us than ever."

The arrangements for founding the George Henry Lewes Studentship at Cambridge had been completed by the middle of September. In November George Eliot returned to London, and in the beginning of the following year her friendship with Mr. Cross became more intimate than before. He gives us the following account of it :

"As the year went on George Eliot began to see all her old friends again. But her life was nevertheless a life of heart-loneliness. Accustomed as she had been for so many years to solitude *à deux*, the want of close companionship continued to be very bitterly felt. She was in the habit of going with me very frequently to the National Gallery and to other exhibitions of pictures, to the British Museum sculptures, and to South Kensington. This constant association engrossed me completely and was a new interest to her.

A bond of mutual dependence had been formed between us. On the 28th March she came down to Weybridge, and stayed till the 30th ; and on the 9th April it was finally decided that our marriage should take place as soon, and as privately, as might be found practicable."

She announced her marriage to her friends, Madame Bodichon, and Mrs. Congreve, only the evening before it took place, saying to the former : " I am going to do what, not very long ago, I should myself have pronounced impossible for me, and therefore I should not wonder at any one else who found my action incomprehensible."

One of the most satisfactory results of her marriage was that it brought about a reconciliation with her brother Isaac, and renewed an intercourse which had long been intermitted. She wrote in answer to him : "Your letter was forwarded to me here, and it was a great joy to me to have your kind words of sympathy, for our long silence has never broken the affection for you which began when we were little ones. My husband, too, was much pleased to read your letter. I have known his family for eleven years, and they have received me amongst them very lovingly. The only point to be regretted in our marriage is that I am much older than he, but his affection has made him choose this lot of caring for me rather than any other of the various lots open to him." They returned to England at the end of July, and George Eliot died on December 22, 1880. Her illness began to declare itself at the end of September, and its progress must be told in her husband's words :

" This attack was a recurrence of the renal disorder of the pre-

vious year. On the 29th of September we went for ten days to
Brighton, as the most accessible place for a bracing change. The
first effects of the sea breezes were encouraging, but the improvement was not maintained. Shortly after our return to Witley, Dr.
Andrew Clark, 'the beloved physician,' came down to consult with
Mr. Parson of Godalming—on 22nd October. From that time there
was gradual but slow improvement, and during November a decided
recovery of strength. But an English autumn was not favourable
to the invalid. Her sensibility to climate influences was extreme.
It will have been noticed in the preceding letters how constantly
change of air and scene was required. I had never seen my wife out
of England, previous to our marriage, except the first time at Rome,
when she was suffering. My general impression, therefore, had
been that her health was always very low, and that she was almost
constantly ailing. Moreover, I had been with her very frequently
during her long, severe illness at Witley in 1879. I was the more
surprised, after our marriage, to find that from the day she set her
feet on Continental soil, till the day she returned to Witley, she was
never ill—never even unwell. She began at once to look many years
younger. During the eleven years of our acquaintance I had never
seen her so strong in health. The greater dryness and lightness of
the atmosphere seemed to have a magical effect. At Paris we spent
our mornings at the Louvre or the Luxembourg, looking at pictures or
sculpture, . . . always fatiguing work. In the afternoon we took long
walks in the Bois, and very often went to the theatre in the evening.
Reading and writing filled in all the interstices of time : yet there
was no consciousness of fatigue. And we had the same experience
at all the places we stayed at in Italy. On our way home, she was
able to take a great deal of walking exercise at Wildbad and Baden.
Decrease of physicial strength coincided exactly with the time of our
return to the damper climate of England. The specific form of
illness did not declare itself until two months later, but her health
was never again the same as it had been on the Continent. Towards
the middle of October she was obliged to keep her bed, but without
restriction as to the amount of reading and talking, which she was
always able to enjoy, except in moments of acute pain."

I well remember the circumstances of her death. On

Monday, December 20th, I was delivering a lecture at
Weybridge, and the chair was taken by a relative of
Mr. Cross. I asked him if he had heard anything lately
of George Eliot and her husband, and he told me that
he had heard from Mr. Cross that morning that his wife
was suffering from a strange attack in the throat, something like croup, very painful, but not dangerous, and
that her recovery was expected in a few days. I went next
day to Windsor to keep my mother's birthday, and a
friend who was to have stayed with us for Christmas did
not arrive at the time expected. He told us when he came
that on his way he had called at 4, Cheyne Walk, Chelsea,
had found Mr. Cross in despair at the sudden death of
his wife, and had remained the night to comfort him. At
six o'clock on Wednesday evening they first knew that
she was dying, and she expired at ten. She was, happily,
unconscious of her approaching end, and indeed had
always anticipated a long life.

I was one of the mourners at her funeral on December
29th. As I entered the lower room in Cheyne Walk, her
portrait, by Sir Frederick Burton, faced me, and brought
back with startling vividness the charm of her living presence. The day was cold and stormy, filled with violent
gusts of wind and rain. During the long drive to High-
gate Cemetery, Mr. William Blackwood, who was with
me, told me the story of her works. Despite the miserable
weather, the churchyard was crowded with men and
women, an orderly and respectful throng, deeply stirred
with sympathy. Among the mourners, the most notice-
able form was that of Isaac Evans, tall and slightly
bent, his features recalling with a striking veracity the

lineaments of the dead. The service in the crowded chapel was impressive, and nowhere more so than when the preacher quoted the words of her well-known hymn, which reminded us that her spirit had joined the choir invisible, "whose music is the gladness of the world." Her portrait hangs over my writing-table at Cambridge, and scarcely a day passes that I do not seek to draw from it some portion of that spiritual strength for which I was so deeply indebted to her during her life.

CHAPTER V.

IT remains for me to sum up in this last chapter the principal characteristics of George Eliot's art, the lines of development which it followed, and the aims which she set herself in working it out. For this purpose her poetry may be set on one side. It was always subordinate to her prose and, as has been maintained in the foregoing pages, was mainly a concentrated form of expression specially adapted to her more subtle and imaginative thoughts. To deal, then, with her novels: Which of them do we rank the highest? It would probably be difficult to get any large number of people to unite in the same conclusion. The popular vote, as shown by the publishers' account books, is, I believe, in favour of "Adam Bede." It is not difficult to understand this. The title of the novel—the names of the first created man and of the first English writer—strikes the keynote of its character. The scene is laid in the heart of the Midlands. The story is a simple tale of a thoughtless boy and a ruined girl—simple yet full of tragic pathos. The deeper thought of the book is expressed in the forms of Puritanism, like all deeper thought in the great mass of English people. It is the

wittiest of George Eliot's novels.   It is written straight
out of her own life.   Adam Bede was her father, Dinah
was her aunt, the name Poyser seems to be compounded
of the names of her mother and her stepmother.   The
story of Hetty was a true one, and may have lain nearer
to her heart than is generally supposed.   All this goes to
justify the popular verdict.   Like the ancient wrestler,
she drew her strength from mother earth, and in no book
did she touch mother earth so closely.

But although this is the popular, it is not the universal
opinion.   Men of letters, I believe, give the palm to
"Silas Marner."   They are attracted by the exquisite
workmanship of the story.   The plot was constructed by
George Eliot out of the merest hint.   The story was
written in haste, at one gush.   It is a perfect gem—a
pure work of art, in which the demands of art have alone
to be considered.   A large class of admirers would give
their vote to "Romola."   It is, as I have said before,
perhaps, the best historical novel ever written.   Replete
with learning, weighted with knowledge in every page,
the finish is so rare that the joints between erudition and
imagination cannot be discovered.   Read it when you
have never been to Florence, it will make you long to go
there ; read it when you have learnt to love Florence, it
will make you love Florence more ; read it when you
have studied the Renaissance, which George Eliot had
studied so deeply, and you will feel its beauties as those
feel the beauties of a symphony of Beethoven who know
the score by heart.   There is the character of Tito, so
special yet so universal, the creature of his own age and
yet the creature of any age, the embodiment of weak sel-

fishness which knows not where it goes, now and ever the most fruitful cause of human misery ; and Romola herself, a saint living in the world, a prototype of Dorothea.   Yet, say others, the book has great inherent faults. All historical novels are inartistic ; they are bad, as historical pictures are bad, as programme music is bad.   No historical picture represents the scene as it actually occurred ; no music ever realized to us the sound of a storm, a nightingale, or a quail.   The armour of erudition encumbers the limbs ; the wise man, like the brave brothers in " Princess Ida," throws it off when he goes into action.   Again, the novel is not a true picture of Italian life.   Men who have lived long in Italy, and have drunk deeply of its spirit, complain that they cannot read the book with pleasure.   The life of Tuscany which it describes is to them a nightmare, a Frankenstein, an artificial monster, not living flesh and blood.

I might quote the highest authority for the superiority of " Middlemarch," in which George Eliot returns to the Midlands.   It is a great prose epic, large in size, commanding in structure, affording an ample space for a great artist to work upon.   Perhaps even more than " Adam Bede " has it become part of the ordinary furniture of our minds, of the current coin of our thoughts.   Casaubon, Will Ladislaw, Mr. Brooke are types which are ever present with us, like Becky Sharpe and Colonel Newcome ; and if Dorothea and Lydgate are more remote, it is because they are rarer characters, not because they are less truly drawn.   " Middlemarch " gives George Eliot the chiefest claim to stand by the side of Shakespeare.   Both drew their inspiration from the same sources, the villages and the country houses which we know so well.

If I am asked the question with which I set out, I always reply—her last novel, "Daniel Deronda." I know well, only too well, the criticisms which have been levelled at the book from its first appearance to the present day. I have become tired and sick of hearing that the characters are unreal, that there is not a man or woman in the story whom you can take away with you and live with. I know that Daniel is thought to be a prig, and the Jew Mordecai a bore; that Gwendolen is thought impossible, and Grandcourt a stage villain; that the language is held to be strained and uncouth, full of far-fetched tropes and metaphors drawn from unfamiliar science. It is said there is no motive power in the action, no reason for the characters behaving as they behave. What rational person can care for the return of the Jews to Palestine? Is a young man who stakes his life on such an issue worthy of five minutes' consideration? Would a handsome young Englishman, brought up as a Christian at a public school or university, be suddenly overjoyed to find that he was a Jew? No, in "Daniel Deronda" thought and learning have usurped the place of art. It belongs to the worst type of all novels, a novel with a tendency. The influence of George Lewes, which may have strengthened his wife's mind at first, has acquired in this a fatal predominance. Biological studies have ruined her fine sensibility. George Eliot has passed her prime. As in the "Transfiguration" of Raphael, we see in "Deronda" the downward movement of a great mind, a movement which, if followed, would have disastrous effect upon the national literature.

With none of this can I agree. To me " Daniel Deronda " is one step further upwards in the career of a soaring genius who was destined, if life was spared, to achieve greater heights than any to which it had yet risen. It is the result of the normal and regular growth of un-rivalled powers which were ever seeking subjects more and more worthy for their exercise. It is as superior to " Adam Bede " as " Hamlet " is superior to " Much Ado About Nothing." It is an effort to realize the highest purposes of art, to seize the strongest passions, the loftiest heights and the lowest depths of human nature. If it fails in execution it is because the task cannot yet be accomplished. But if the work is ever to be done, the way must be paved by partial failure. It is better to have tried and failed, than never to have tried at all.

Let us trace the development of George Eliot's art in its more outward aspects. Novel-writing did not come naturally to her. She did not, like Currer Bell, spend her girlhood in " making " stories, conscious only of the pleasure which it gave her, and unconscious of their excellence. Nor did she, like George Sand, sit down at nightfall and be halfway through a novel by next morning, the plot of which developed as she wrote. Like Milton, she was from the first a student. The first work she thought of writing, let us remember, was a synopsis of ecclesiastical history, demanding nothing but great learn-ing, clear thought, and untiring industry and ingenuity. Her best mental training, in her own opinion, which

I have before recorded, came from the labour of trans-
lating Strauss's "Life of Jesus," and of finding the
exact English equivalents for subtle German particles.
For five-and-thirty years she laboriously acquired knowledge, became accomplished in at least five languages
besides her own, learned all she could of this, but kept
the force and flower of her mind for philosophy, and
especially for that region of philosophy which borders on
religion. Throughout her life she went back to the
Greek sources of inspiration in preference to seeking it
in the clash and play of human passion.

Any one who had followed her intellectual growth up
to the publication of "Scenes of Clerical Life" would
never have guessed that it would have resulted in fiction.
She might become a great essayist, a great philosopher, an
historian, or a preacher like her aunt Dinah, but a novelist
never. Thus the Brays, who knew her mind intimately,
never guessed that she was the mysterious unknown, and
were surprised when they heard it. So also with her style.
The careful student of her letters can trace the unity of
the style from her earliest writings to the end, but this
will not be apparent to the hasty reader. Her first
letters are precise, prim, even priggish, if I may use
the word. She is pedantically exact in grammar; if
she has learnt a new word she uses it to show that she
knows it. There is from the first a remarkable just-
ness and accuracy of expression, the fitting of the glove
which leaves no fold or wrinkle, an insight into the
depths of thought which discovers the truest representation of it, a vivid accuracy of description; but there is
nothing that shows the coming novelist. There is no

dramatic power, there is no humour. Indeed, the
humour of George Eliot, its nature and development,
would demand an essay by itself. What can be more
irresistible than the humour of "Adam Bede," or of
the "Mill on the Floss"? Yet long and intimately
as I knew George Eliot, I never remember to have
heard her say a humorous thing, nor have I ever heard
a humorous saying of hers repeated by those who
knew her better than I did. There is scarcely any
humour in her letters. When she writes to her stepson,
with every effort to sympathize with his studies and
amusements, there is no humour, and yet a word of Aunt
Glegg's would have made any boy ripple with laughter.
I used to attribute this persistent earnestness to an
exaggerated self-command, to a moral nature which kept
a tight rein on all temptation to sarcasm, conscious of
the scathing force with which it might be exercised. But
had humour been natural to her, there would have been
evidence of it in familiar letters, and fragments of table-
talk would have been garnered by faithful disciples.
No; her mind was ever deeply serious, overweighted
with a sense of the importance of every action and of
every word, indeed of every influence which she might
exercise upon her fellow-creatures. She gave every
comer of her best, and spoke sometimes of her novel-
writing as if it were a frivolous pursuit compared
with the histories and philosophies of her less gifted
friends.

Yet her capacity for fiction had not escaped the pene-
tration of those who knew her best. George Lewes
knew that she could describe and analyze, but doubted

whether she possessed dramatic power. A great philosopher, one of her most intimate associates, had always told her that her strength would lie in novel-writing. At last, on returning to Richmond after a long absence, he heard that his advice had been taken and that she had begun. The first "Scenes of Clerical Life" had been written. Even then she moved timidly and with caution in the domain of imagination. The first stories were reproductions of her own experience; places and persons were so described as to be easily recognized, names were scarcely altered. Yet she had prepared herself for the analysis of character by careful study. I have seen a copy of Benjamin Constant's "Adolphe," a novel of the minutest self-inspection, interlined and marked by her in every page, and thumbed so as almost to fall in pieces. From such elements were those tales produced which shook so rapidly the heart of England. Based on a wealth of thought and learning which none of her readers could rival or understand, they dealt with the joys and sorrows of simple everyday men and women. If the delicate half-lights were unperceived by critics and admirers, the main outlines were struck with such vigour and decision that he who ran could comprehend.

From the first there was a tone of sadness in her stories. She set herself to describe ordinary life and to sympathize with common joys and sorrows. She had no respect for that art which deals only with polite society, and overlooks the struggles of the humdrum people with whom we are perpetually in contact. Nor did she seek approval by making her heroes happy. We have been told by experienced playwrights that the catastrophe of a play has much to do with its success. There are some stories which the public will not allow to end unhappily, however much such an end may be demanded by the truth of art. Deep in human nature lies the instinct of compensation, the confidence that everything must be for the best; that misery in this world is certain to be made right in the next; and that very probably in our present condition there will be something to set off on the other side. George Eliot's nature rejected with scorn this easy method of making things pleasant. She knew too well that everything is not always for the best; she regarded this unfounded confidence as one of the most fruitful sources of immoral action. She was never tired of repeating that the good and evil which exist in the world are the outcome of good and bad actions done by generations of human beings. Our lives are certain to add something to the sum on one side or the other; let us be on our guard, not only that our actions are positively good, but that they are so directed as to interfere as little as possible with the good which others are trying to effect. The worst evil is often wrought by those who are free from the most repugnant qualities. Stupidity, and, above all, an easy, self-indulgent disposition, may bring ruin on its possessor, and on all who come into contact with him. Such men are favourites in the world, and are not considered to be bad. They are described as well-meaning, and as "no man's enemy but their own." Yet Goethe and George Eliot warn us with persistent iteration that by characters such as this the best lives are wasted. One thoughtless moment of Arthur

Donnithorne brings ruin and death to Hetty. Tito sinks by slow gradations of easy selfishness into a villain and a murderer. Edward, in the Wahlverwandschaften of Goethe, ruins characters far nobler than his own. Werther is of the same type, but the glamour of the artist has endowed him with such attractiveness that he rather invited imitators than gave a warning. George Eliot did not intend her novels to wear a robe of sombre melancholy. Nothing was more foreign to her than the belief that most lives must be failures; no feeling would she less have desired to generate than despair of good and distrust of effort. Her personal influence was stimulating; to many souls she was a prophetess, inspiring them with hope for the struggle of life, ordering their careers, marshalling their forces, making them see the honour of a humble task and an obscure function. Her voice was like that of a great captain which cheers not only those who are in the forefront of the conflict, but those who, set to guard the women and the stuff, hear the roar of warfare from afar. There lay undoubtedly a deep gloom in the recesses of her own nature, and this dark background may have appeared in her writings in spite of herself. She once said to her friend with deep solemnity that she regarded it a wrong and misery that she ever had been born. But her self-command would have crushed this pessimism had she supposed that it could have injuriously affected others.

She was also profoundly conscious of the little thought and value which many people set on life, how little they estimate the result of their actions in themselves and others. She feared that this was encouraged by the

current theology, which looked only to future retribu-
tion, to reward and punishment in a heaven and hell
external to ourselves, to a future state where all mistakes
and accidents of this life would be comfortably set right.
Let us think more of this life, she would say; here is
heaven and hell enough for us. We have no certain
knowledge of the details of a future life; this life we do
know, and by care and watchfulness we may repress its
evil and increase its good. To inculcate the importance
of every action of our lives, whether as affecting the lives
of others, or by the invincible force of habit determining
our own; the momentous issues of the thoughts and
emotions which slowly build up the human character,
and which, long concealed from all eyes, suddenly leap
out in the light of unexpected action; such was the
kernel of her moral teaching.

> "Let thy chief terror be of thine own soul:
> There, 'mid the throng of hurrying desires
> That trample o'er the dead to seize their spoil,
> Lurks vengeance, footless, irresistible
> As exhalation laden with slow death;
> And o'er the fairest troop of captured joys
> Breathes pallid pestilence."

If the lives of Dorothea, of Maggie Tulliver, of
Romola, are failures, it is not because George Eliot
wishes to teach that most lives are and must be failures,
but because she believes that such failures are pre-
ventible, and that it is our duty to prevent them as far
as possible. We cannot ourselves have high destinies or
momentous influence; but are we not surrounded by
those who have or might have? Do we not by our

narrowness, by our selfishness or our careless thought-
lessness, spoil lives created for the noblest purpose?

I know what I have said to be true from repeated
conversations with her on this topic. I remember, one
summer afternoon in Windsor Park, many years ago,
I found myself for a moment alone with her, and
ventured to pour into her ears the difficulties which were
then assailing me, the struggle between the demands of
the life of self-culture and the life of self-sacrifice, which
is the common malady of youthful minds, or was so at
least a quarter of a century ago. She turned upon me with
the eager glance of a prophetess, and said, " I know all
you mean, I have felt it all myself;" and then followed
a flood of eloquence upon the purpose of life, and the
necessities of social effort, and the nobility of humble
duties, which from that moment put an end to my unrest
and laid the germs of content. I remember also a
dinner party at Cambridge, where she discoursed with
earnest self-abandonment into my private ear of the
solemnities of this life, and the danger of always grasping
at a life beyond. But this train of thought is the keynote
of the earliest of her published essays, the review of
Young's " Night Thoughts," or, as she calls it, " Worldliness and Other-worldliness."

Young, she says in this, has no conception of religion
as anything else than egoism turned heavenward.
Religion, he tells us, is

" Ambition, pleasure, and the love of gain, directed towards the
joys of the future life instead of the present. He never changes his
level so as to see beyond the region of mere selfishness. Virtue

with Young must always squint—must never look straight towards the immediate object of emotion and effect. Thus, if a man risks perishing in the snow himself rather than forsake a weaker comrade, he must do this either because his hopes and fears are directed to another world, or because he desires to applaud himself afterwards."

On the other hand, George Eliot says—

"I am just and honest, not because I expect to live in another world, but because, having felt the pain of injustice and dishonesty towards myself, I have a fellow feeling with other men who would suffer the same pains if I were unjust or dishonest towards them. Why should I give my neighbour short weight in this world because there is not another world in which I should have nothing to weigh out to him? I am honest because I don't like to inflict evil on others in this life, not because I am afraid of evil to myself in another. It is a pang to me to witness the suffering of a fellow-being, and I feel his suffering the more because he is mortal, because his life is so short, and I would have it, if possible, filled with happiness, and not misery. In some minds the deep pathos lying in the thought of human mortality—that we are here for a little while and then vanish away; that this earthly life is all that is given to our loved ones, and to our many suffering fellow-men—lies nearer the fountains of moral emotion than the conception of extended existence."

I trust that I have said nothing to imply that the tendency of George Eliot's teaching was towards unbelief or indifference. Her nature was intensely religious, she had been brought up in surroundings of the most earnest piety, even if accompanied by a narrow dogmatism. The tenderness and delicacy of her nature would have forbidden her to write a word which could have weakened the faith of a single believing soul. I once heard George Lewes urging her to declare herself, to take a side in religious thought, to bear a part in the conflict against current belief, for which so many were enduring unpopularity and ostracism. She refused and appealed to me. It was, if I remember right, between the publication of "Middlemarch" and "Deronda." Why should she hurt the numbers who loved and trusted her through her writings? Why, if she deeply sympathized with their faith, even if she had ceased to hold it, should she carry the weapons of scorn and refutation against the host of ideas which were bred of purity and virtue? The first thing to teach, she had written to me, is reverence, reverence for the hard-won beliefs of many struggling ages. The answer to her husband's appeal was given in "Deronda," a book in which there is not a word of reproach against the most childlike faith, but where the great mysteries of revelation from which Christianity derives its origin are held up to admiration, preserved throughout the centuries by the joint guardianship of obedience and race.

This, then, I take to be the key-note of George Eliot's art :—to paint the lives of those she saw about her, to describe their joys and sorrows, their successes and failures, and, by insisting on the deep importance of this world, to teach us to hinder as little as possible the good which is burgeoning around us. This, I say, is the germ; but how did this art develop? She died in the fulness of her powers. There is no failure in grasp of intellect or cunning of style. Gwendolen is as complicated and difficult a character as she ever painted. Is it not reasonable to believe that, in the maturity of her mind and the height of her influence, she would in writing "Deronda" have braced herself to a supreme effort, have nerved herself to satisfy the claims of the highest art, and to soar with no common or slender pinion beyond the Aonian mount?

We have said that from the first she sought for inspiration in the joys and sorrows of ordinary people. But what are their joys and sorrows? The commonest passions we know are love and revenge. They beat in the breast of every savage, nay, of every brute. Heine's old song, " She was lovable, and he loved her ; He was not lovable, and she loved him not," is chanted in various cadences every moment of our lives. What are the outward motives of the most famous tragedies ? In the "Agamemnon" of Æschylus a soldier comes home from the wars. In his ten years' absence his wife has formed another attachment. When he arrives she receives him kindly, invites him to take a warm bath, envelops him in a complicated bathing-towel, and cuts him down with a hatchet. It is true that he has killed her daughter some years before, and has brought home with him a lovely waiting-maid, of whom her mistress might be jealous. But these are only excuses, the plot has been long arranged. Clytemnestra does not intend to desert her paramour Ægisthus for her husband Agamemnon. It is an affair of every day ; we may read it any week in the police news, or hear of it in the purlieus of our great cities. If the plot does not always end in a murder, it is because Agamemnon is often content to solace himself with Cassandra. Again, in the "Medea," an adventurous traveller in unknown and distant lands takes to himself a wife of the country. She was very useful to him with the natives, and doubtless did her best to ensnare him. She was a hasty, ill-tempered woman, not like a European, and given to magic arts. The traveller returns rich and famous; the beautiful princess of the wealthiest city in the world falls in love with him and marries him. The dark-haired stranger rages like a mad woman. She poisons her rival and kills her two children to revenge herself on their father. In England she would be tried for murder, and very often is. In Greece she happily escaped in a carriage drawn by winged dragons. Again, in "Faust," the action of deepest interest, although the Germans call it an episode, is the ruin of Gretchen. A simple girl, dazzled by splendid gifts and promises, absorbed by a personality more radiant than any of which she had dreamed, falls, repents, kills her mother and her child. "Yet everything that drove me on was goodness and was love alone." What is this but the story of Hetty— a story to which every one of us could find a parallel? "Sie war die erste nicht" ("She was not the first") says Mephisto, to the despairing Faust: nor unhappily was she the last. It is the very simplicity of the pathos, its appeal to universal experience, which gives the story of Margaret its hold on the hearts of men. Read or acted, spoken or sung, treated by Spohr, Gounod, Berlioz, or Boito, it draws tears from men and women of every country.

But is art never to rise beyond these simple passions? A complex civilization may produce great criminals, but it is also the parent of acts of heroism which are less likely to be found in a simpler society. A statesman

is filled from earliest youth with the idea of creating
a country, of realizing what generations of dreaming
patriots have yearned for during expectant centuries.
He trains himself in silence for his task, he dares not
whisper his purpose for fear it should be thwarted, he
learns by patient self-command how to restrain himself
at the moment when action is tempting but may be
dangerous.   He has the flash of the eagle eye which
tells him when to take the tiger spring; he dies prema-
turely, worn out with labour, but his work is accomplished
and lives after him.   A philosopher conceives in boy-
hood the outlines of a great constructive system, he
knows that it will take a lifetime to work out, and he
willingly gives his life to the cause.   There is a fire of
heroism in the conception, in the first beginning, which
needs no patience to sustain it, but the highest qualities
of mind and heart are needed for the prolonged per-
sistence of weeks, months, and years.   Are not these
actions as truly heroic as any scene which struts the
stage in all the pomp of circumstance?   Is not the
devotion to an ideal as true a passion as the wooing of
a village maiden?   Is not the great traveller and dis-
coverer as true a hero as the great conqueror?   May
not Livingstone stand by the side of Alexander?   And
surely these modern passions have their tragic catastro-
phes no less than their simple antitypes.   What can be
more tragic than the fate of Gordon, falling at the
moment when success seemed certain?   He was, we
may say, a martyr to duty, to military obedience, but
also to that love of the weak and oppressed, to that
hatred of slavery which could not exist in a barbaric nature.

Napoleon, who offers in his powerful and complex personality many grand subjects for art, saw this clearly. In a conversation with the Comte de Segur, he complained that poets showed no enterprise in drawing from the rich material with which the grandeur of the modern world supplied them. "What," he said, "can be more tragic than the struggle in the mind of a wise and powerful ruler when he is called upon to decide whether he shall do something which he knows to be essential, and to be just, but which bears an outward appearance of tyranny and hardship, and will cover his name with ignominy?" This was his view of the execution of the Duc d'Enghien. Art can deal easily enough with the fate of the unfortunate young prince, treacherously seized, hurried to the capital, shot on a grey morning in the ditch of a fortress. Such a scene can be easily described so as to touch all hearts. "More tragic," Napoleon said, "more worthy of the highest art, is the struggle in the mind of the sovereign who feels all the pathos with which men will invest his victim, and the ignominy which they will heap upon himself, and yet chooses wisdom and reprobation instead of weakness and applause?" Who amongst us has not wept over Mary Queen of Scots?—yet we have no tears for Elizabeth or Burleigh. A friend of mine, an ardent Liberal, once wrote a tragedy called "Cromwell," in which all our sympathy was to be evoked for that great man. We who read it discovered that all the pathos had been given to Charles I., and we would willingly have condemned Cromwell to the fate of his victim. The artist, we allow, should describe what he sees and

what he knows; the subjects with which he is habitually
in contact. But are our most intimate friends Clytem-
nestras or Medeas? and if there is even in the best
men a strain of lower nature, are we to fix our eyes
on that, and not on those qualities which give value
to the friendship of our friend?

Such, in my opinion, was the development of George
Eliot's art. She always described those whom she
knew. But Milly Barton, sweet and touching as she
is, appealing to all hearts, is not a Dorothea or a
Romola. Milly, propped up by pillows in the early
morning mending her children's stockings, is a far
simpler character than Romola, full of ancient learning
and enthusiasm, casting herself upon the guidance of
Savonarola. In all these types there is a progression.
We are taught to feel that the highest forms of
heroism are still with us and amongst us if we would
but recognize them. Dorothea, she tells us, was a
modern St. Theresa. Fedalma, the Spanish gypsy, who
sacrifices everything for her race, was suggested, she
informs us, by Titian's picture of the youthful Virgin,
conscious that she carried in her bosom the destinies of
the world.

But art in attempting to describe these higher passions
has great difficulties to deal with. It must appeal to a
smaller audience. Many more are touched by a simple
tale of every-day experience than by complicated
struggles of mind or character. So a sweet-toned ballad
will always have more to listen to it than a quartett of
Beethoven, although the last may contain a hundredfold
more melody, and be destined to live long after the

ballad is forgotten. The analogy of music might be pressed more closely. There is scarcely a masterpiece of music of the highest rank which was not at the time of its production condemned as complicated, artificial, unmelodious, and unintelligible. Mozart's great quartetts were returned by the engraver as so full of mistakes that they could not be printed. The best works of Beethoven were not performed till forty years after his death. Some of the best works of Bach have never been performed at all. Much of the popularity of Handel is due to his simplicity and straightforwardness; and we have been told by a great critic that a capital defect in Shakespeare is his fondness for obvious characters.

Another great difficulty with those who attempt to extend the domain of art lies in the poverty of language. The language of ordinary passion is well known; it is ready to our hand, and strikes directly to our hearts. The death scene of Milly Barton, the conversation between Faust and Margaret, are expressed in the simplest words and produce their full effects. The moment this domain is left the instrument fails. We have no simple vocabulary in which we can paint the inspiration of Dorothea, the long-drawn yearning of Mordecai, the chivalrous self-devotion of Deronda, or even the artistic conscience of Klesmer. If we merely describe or analyze we cease to be passionate; if we would be passionate we must borrow the language of passion, but we must transmute its meaning. We must change it so as to apply not to bodies, but to souls, not to realities, but to abstractions. We can no longer speak with forcible directness, we must use metaphor, and metaphor kills.

In this we shall find an extenuation and an excuse for one of the chief transgressions with which George Eliot has been charged. Her husband, it is said, had a baneful influence over her. Absorbed in science he led her away from art, her language becomes more and more unintelligible; we find long periodic sentences, far-fetched allusions, recondite terms, scientific analogies, till what ought to be a novel reads like a paper at the British Association. The charge against Lewes is unfair. Her very first published essay begins with a scientific metaphor. To study men as a branch of natural history was the inherent tendency of her mind. But as her characters became more complex, and their struggles more subtle, they can only be made intelligible at all by metaphor. Scientific metaphor was the best and truest instrument at her hand, and no one can deny that she wielded it with extraordinary power and success.

If the development of George Eliot's art led her to place before us complex characters, stirred by passions which are not familiar to the mass of mankind, the development of Goethe's art led him into a similar although a slightly divergent path. His earliest works were characterized by their preciseness and directness. In the "Sorrows of Werther" the intractable German tongue is made to speak with a melodious softness unknown to any language since the Greek of Plato. The style is simple and easy. Werther pours out his complaint with childish *naiveté*. In the more tragic parts the pathos is produced by the means nearest at hand.

The description of Werther's death and funeral is a mere transcript of Kestner's letter describing the death and funeral of the young Jerusalem who, as everybody knows, was Werther's prototype. In "Goetz von Berlichingen" we see the same qualities applied to the portrayal of a massive character. In this play the unities of time and place are recklessly disregarded, the scene shifts from one spot to another to the despair of stage-managers. The characters speak in short, pithy sentences, they come on without preparation, they say a few words and are off again. Let me give a specimen from the fifth act, in the very agony of the climax. The scene lies in the courtyard of an inn. The previous scene has shown us the judges of the secret tribunal meeting in a narrow, gloomy vault. The next scene will show us Goetz and his wife Elizabeth in the tower of his castle at Heilbronn. Here we have Maria and her page hastening to her brother Goetz; and this is what they say: *M.* "The horses have rested enough, we will away, Lerse." *L.* "Stay till morning; the night is too wild." *M.* "Lerse, I have no rest till I have seen my brother. Let us away. The weather becomes clearer; we may expect a fine day." *L.* "As you please."

That is all. Yet every word carries with it the sense of hurried, anxious flight. So in the first part of "Faust," the more dramatic parts, and those which were earliest composed, have the same qualities — they are the quintessence of dramatic simplicity and force. Yet what did De Quincey, the great English critic, tell us about Goethe some fifty years ago?

He says that his reputation is founded on his obscurity,
and that it cannot last. Goethe had the art, even the
cunning, to write unintelligibly, and to excite the
curiosity of readers as to what he meant. As long as
there is something to find out he is studied: when
everything is cleared up, and it is known either what
he means, or that he has no meaning, he will be read
no more.

But what produced this change? What transmuted the
clear, sharp language of the gifted boy into the obscure
and dreamy dialect of the mature man? Why did the
author of the first part of " Faust " ever write a second
part? It was because he strove after the development
of art; because he wished to apply it to worthier
subjects. Werther is a foolish, sentimental youth who
shoots himself because he cannot gratify a hopeless
passion. Goetz is a simple knight of the Middle Ages,
rough and rugged as the ashlar of his castle walls.
These characters spoke to Goethe's generation as the
style speaks to us still: one was typical of the men of
the eighteenth century which was passing away, the
other of the new-born strength of awakened Germany.
But compare them with Faust. Here, in the less
dramatic and more philosophical parts, we are brought
face to face with the problems of our own day. The
opening soliloquy, the struggle of Faust with the temptation of his lower nature, his dialogues with Wagner and
with Mephisto, are all modern. They appeal to us as if
they were written yesterday. And yet they are very
obscure. The language is difficult in German, unintelligible in a translation. And if this is the case even

in the early Faust, what shall we say of Goethe's later writings, of the second part of "Wilhelm Meister," of Pandora, of the Xenien, the proverbs, the West-ostliche Divan, the second part of " Faust"?

The German language has a power, which English does not possess, of lending itself to the correct expression of the most complicated abstract ideas. Its malleability, its comprehensiveness, the ease with which its component parts can be thrown together and kneaded into new shapes at the will of the writer, makes it an unrivalled instrument in the hand of a man of genius. If Goethe wished to exhibit recondite passions, he need not, like George Eliot, have recourse to metaphor, he could extend the compass of his own language at his will. If he tried—what George Eliot did not attempt— to deal with the universal instead of the particular, to say things true for all time instead of for his time, applicable to all men and not to one man, dealing sometimes with all nature or with the whole universe—again the material was ready for him. He had a speech which would obey his most soaring fancies, even as the Greek language lends itself to the wild imaginings of the Alexandrian Platonists. Goethe used this liberty to the utmost. He who had taught German to speak with limpid music in " Werther" and with rugged force in "Goetz," preferred in the maturity of his might to utter abstractions of which few discerned the meaning, and which many declared to have no meaning. Yet they are becoming current coin to our generation. The second part of "Faust" is acted in many a German city, and the press of Germany teems with cheap editions of its great poet, not with his masterpiece only, but with everything he ever wrote, his scientific treatises included.

I may now come back to the question with which I began. Which of George Eliot's novels do we rank the highest ? If I have at all carried my readers with me in my reasoning, they will agree with me that there is a gradual progression from first to last, that during her twenty-five years of literary production she was ever conceiving deeper views of the problem of life, and was filled with a stronger sense of the responsibilities of her mission. She strove more and more to grasp the difficulties of complex characters such as she met in the course of her London life, and such as she learnt to have more sympathy for ; to express not only their appearance and their manners, but the very inmost secrets and battles of their hearts. In one of her essays there is a criticism of Dickens, which has been but little noticed. She says :—

" We have one great novelist who is gifted with the utmost power of rendering the external traits of our town population ; and if he could give us their psychological character, their conceptions of life, and their emotions with the same truth as their dress and manners, his books would be the greatest contribution art has ever made to the awakening of social sympathies. But while he can copy Mrs. Plornish's colloquial style with the delicate accuracy of a true picture, while there is the same startling inspiration in his description of the gestures and phrases of ' Boots ' as in the speeches of Shakespeare's mobs and numskulls, he scarcely ever passes from the humorous and external to the emotional and the tragic without becoming as transcendent in his unreality as he was a moment before in his artistic truthfulness."

George Eliot never failed to deal with the inner nature
of her characters. But what a chasm there is between
her first story and her last! In the "Sad Fortunes of
the Reverend Amos Barton" there are but few characters,
and those of the humblest kind. An underbred clergyman of very ordinary appearance and capacity, a loving
wife and mother, a countess who had been a governess,
her brother a retired tradesman, a sympathetic neighbour,
an outspoken country servant—these make up the whole
of the *dramatis personæ*. Others are indicated with marvellous truth, but they hardly enter into the action. They are
all simple characters, such as may be met with any day
in any country town. Compared with this, " Deronda "
assumes the proportions of an epic poem. It is of
great length, and the plot is of rare complexity. There
are episodes which might be detached from the main
action. The simplest characters, the Gascoignes and
the Meyricks, have a touch of rareness and elevation ;
whereas the main actors are played upon by the stormiest
passion which can influence humanity in these modern
days. How complicated is the character of Gwendolen,
how difficult to grasp, her feet on the well-known
ground of vanity and ambitious selfishness, yet endowed
with a nature which led her at once to acknowledge the
supremacy of Deronda, and yield herself to his guidance. Myra, a tender plant reared among the worst
surroundings, charming Deronda as the pearl of womanhood, yet in her despair tempted to suicide as Gwendolen
was to murder ; Mordecai, the embodiment of a strange
religion, his frail life at once consumed and sustained
by an absorbing yearning ; Deronda, far different, indeed,

to the ordinary product of a public school or a university,
yet so like nature that his piototype has often been
recognized ; Klesmer, the embodiment of German
culture, so little sympathetic to Englishmen ; Deronda's
mother, so powerfully drawn, a fiery nature well fitted
for the weird fortunes of her youth ; Sir Hector, now
the trusted man of common sense, with the romance of
his young life buried deep beneath its ashes :—all these
characters, created, not only in their external appearance, but in their inmost souls, and woven together in
an intricacy of plot which is the true representation of
real life, such as few authors have the courage to describe,
just as few painters dare to paint with realistic accuracy
the true colours of a glowing sunset.

This, as it is the sum and glory of George Eliot's art,
is also one of the great masterpieces of our literature.
But it is not a book which he who runs may read, and
it may be better understood fifty years hence than it is
at the present day.   It deals with persons and problems
which are only possible in a highly civilized society, and
become more common as civilization advances.   Literature began with Homer, with strife and battles, the
virtues and the vices of semi-savage tribes.   Human
nature is there, but human nature in germ.   The Greeks
of the Homeric age are with us still ; they are to be
found in South Africa and the Soudan ; we have spent
several millions in killing them with Remington rifles
and Gatling guns.   But you will not find amongst them
a Faust, a Wilhelm Meister, a Deronda, or a Gwendolen.
Living art must deal with the circumstances which
environ it, with the deepest problems of advanced

humanity, not only with the joys and sorrows common to all human beings. To do this well and worthily is the privilege of the highest genius, and it was to this stupendous task that two of the greatest writers of this century set themselves in the maturity of their powers. The attempt to compass this, perhaps the partial failure, will link together indissolubly for future ages the names of Goethe and George Eliot.

THE END.

INDEX.

Cross, Mr., George Eliot's husband and biographer, 13, 120, 134-138; quoted, 17, 85, 125, 135, 136-137
Cumming, Dr., George Eliot's opinion of, 36-37

D.

"Daniel Deronda," preparation for, 94, 115, 116; its object, 94; composition, 120 – 121; Jewish element, 122-124; reception, 124; claim to be considered the best of the novels, 143-144, 164-167
Deutsch, Mr. E., 90, 122
Dickens, George Eliot's opinion of his work, 164
Dorking, 85
Dresden, 55-56
Durade, Mons. and Mdme., 31, 72-73, 84, 113

E.

Eliot George (Mary Ann Evans), present views of her work, 11-12; birth, 13; father and family, 13-14; removal to Griff, near Nuneaton, 15-16; mother, 16-17; early days and influences at home and at school, and early traits of character, 16-22; removal to Coventry, 22; life there, 22-24; dispute with her father on religious subjects, 24; views on conformity, 24-25; translates the "Leben Jesu" of Strauss, 25-28; letters at this period,

28-29; death of her father, 29-30; foreign tour and residence at Geneva, 30-32; reviews Mackay's "Progress of the Intellect," 32; removes to Mr. Chapman's house as assistant editor of the *Westminster Review*, 33; friendship with Mr. Herbert Spencer and Mr. Lewes, 33-34; contributions to *Westminster Review*, 34-37; removes to Cambridge Street, Hyde Park, 37; union with Mr. Lewes, 37-40; retires from *Westminster Review*, 37; translates Feuerbach's "Essence of Christianity," 38; goes abroad with Mr. Lewes, 38, 40-41; settles at Richmond, 42; magazine articles, 42; translates Spinoza's "Ethics," 43; "Scenes of Clerical Life" ("Amos Barton," "Mr. Gilfil's Love-Story," and "Janet's Repentance"), 44-53; visit to Munich and Dresden, 54-56; "Adam Bede," 54-65; "The Mill on the Floss" begun, 65; removal to Wandsworth, 66; "The Lifted Veil," 67-68; "The Mill on the Floss," 68-74; difference between earlier and later novels, 71; a sketch of herself, 72; visit to Italy, 74-75; the idea of "Romola" results from visit to Florence, 75-77; removal to Harewood Square and then to Blandford Square, 77; "Silas Marner," 77-80; complaints of ill-health, 78; "Romola," 80-88; second visit to Florence, 80-81; "The Spanish

BIBLIOGRAPHY.

BY

JOHN P. ANDERSON

(British Museum).

I. WORKS.

The Works of George Eliot. (Cabinet edition.) 20 vols. Edinburgh [printed] and London, 1878-80, 8vo.

Novels of George Eliot. (Illustrated edition.) 6 vols. London, Edinburgh [printed], 1867 [-78], 8vo.

Complete Poems of George Eliot. With introductory notice by Matthew Browne. Special limited edition, with illustrations. Boston [1889], 8vo.

Scenes of Clerical Life and Silas Marner. Edinburgh [printed] and London, 1863, 8vo.

Adam Bede. 3 vols. Edinburgh, 1859, 8vo.

Adam Bede. Seventh edition. 2 vols. Edinburgh, 1859, 12mo.

——Tenth edition. Edinburgh [printed] and London, 1862, 8vo.

——New edition. Edinburgh [printed] and London, 1867, 8vo.

——New edition. Edinburgh [printed] and London [1873], 8vo.

Agatha. [A poem.] London, 1869, 8vo.

Appeared originally in the *Atlantic Monthly* for August 1869. Reprinted with the *Legend of Jubal*, etc., in 1874.

Armgart (*Macmillan's Magazine*, vol. 24, 1871, pp. 161-187).

Reprinted with the *Legend of Jubal*, etc., in 1874.

Brother Jacob. (*Cornhill Maga-
zine*, vol. x., 1864, pp. 1-32.)
Reprinted with *Silas Marner* and
the *Lifted Veil* in a volume of the
"Works," 1878.
A College Breakfast Party. (*Mac-
millan's Magazine*, vol. 38,
1878, pp. 161-179.)
Included with the *Legend of
Jubal*, etc., in a volume of the
"Works," 1879.
Daniel Deronda. 4 vols. Edin-
burgh and London, 1876, 8vo.
——New edition. 4 vols. Edin-
burgh [printed] and London,
1876, 8vo.
George Eliot's Life, as related
in her letters and journals.
Arranged and edited by her
husband, J. W. Cross. 3 vols.
Edinburgh and London, 1885,
8vo.
——Cabinet edition. 3 vols.
Edinburgh [1886], 8vo.
Essays and Leaves from a
Note-Book. By George Eliot.
[Edited by C. L. Lewes.]
Edinburgh, 1884, 8vo.
Felix Holt, the Radical. 3 vols.
Edinburgh [printed], London,
1866, 8vo.
——New edition. 2 vols. Edin-
burgh [printed], London, 1866,
8vo.
——Another edition. 2 vols.
Leipzig, 1867, 16mo.
Vols. 897, 898 of the Tauchnitz
Collection of British Authors.
——Another edition. Edinburgh,
1868, 8vo.
——Cabinet edition. 2 vols.
Edinburgh, 1878, 8vo.
How Lisa loved the King. With
new illustrations. Philadelphia,
1883, 4to.
Appeared originally in *Black-
wood's Edinburgh Magazine*, or

May 1869. Reprinted with the
Legend of Jubal, etc., in 1874.
Impressions of Theophrastus Such.
Edinburgh and London, 1879,
8vo.
The Legend of Jubal, and other
Poems. Edinburgh, 1874, 8vo.
"The Legend of Jubal" appeared
originally in *Macmillan's Magazine*,
vol. xxii., 1870.
"The Lifted Veil." A short
story. (*Blackwood's Edinburgh
Magazine*, July 1859.)
Included with *Silas Marner* and
Brother Jacob in a volume of the
"Works," 1878.
Middlemarch, a study of pro-
vincial life. 4 vols. Edinburgh,
1871-72, 8vo.
——New edition. 4 vols. Edin-
burgh [printed], London, 1873,
8vo.
——New edition. Edinburgh
[printed], London, 1874, 8vo.
The Mill on the Floss. 3 vols.
Edinburgh and London, 1860,
8vo.
——New edition. 2 vols. Edin-
burgh [printed] and London,
1860, 8vo.
——Fifth edition, Edinburgh,
1862, 8vo.
——New edition. Edinburgh,
1867, 8vo.
——New edition. 2 vols. Edin-
burgh, 1878, 12mo.
Romola. London, 1863, 8vo.
Appeared originally in the *Corn-
hill Magazine*, from July 1862 to
August 1863.
——Another edition. 2 vols.
Leipzig, 1863, 16mo.
Vols. 682, 683 of the Tauchnitz
Collection of British Authors.
——Illustrated edition. London,
1865, 8vo.
——Another edition. With illus-
trations by Sir F. Leighton.
2 vols. London, 1880, 4to.

Scenes of Clerical Life. 2 vols. Edinburgh, 1858, 8vo.
Originally published in *Blackwood's Magazine*, from Jan. to Nov. 1857, the series comprising "The Sad Fortunes of the Reverend Amos Barton," "Mr. Gilfil's Love Story," and "Janet's Repentance."
——Second edition. 2 vols. Edinburgh [printed] and London, 1859, 8vo.
——Third edition. 2 vols. Edinburgh, 1860, 8vo.
——New edition. Edinburgh, 1868, 8vo.
Silas Marner: the Weaver of Raveloe. Edinburgh [printed] and London, 1861, 8vo.
——Seventh edition. Edinburgh, 1861, 8vo.
——Another edition. Mobile, 1863, 8vo.
——New edition. Edinburgh, 1868, 8vo.
The Spanish Gypsy, a poem. Edinburgh [printed] and London, 1868, 8vo.
——Second edition. Edinburgh [printed] and London, 1868, 8vo.
——Third edition. Edinburgh [printed], London, 1868, 8vo.
——Fifth edition. Edinburgh, 1875, 8vo.

The Essence of Christianity. By L. Feuerbach. Translated from the second German edition by Marian Evans. London, 1854, 12mo.
No. vi. of "Chapman's Quarterly Series."
——Second edition. London, 1881, 8vo.
Vol. xv. of the "English and Foreign Philosophical Library."
The Life of Jesus, critically examined by Dr. D. F. Strauss. Translated from the fourth

German edition [by Marian Evans]. 3 vols. London, 1846, 8vo.

II. MISCELLANEOUS.

Westminster Review—
Mackay's "Progress of the Intellect," vol. 54, 1851, pp. 353-368.
Carlyle's "Life of Sterling," vol. 1 N.S., 1852, pp. 247-251.
Woman in France—Madame de Sablé, vol. 6 N.S., 1854, pp. 448-473.
Prussia and Prussian Policy (Stahr), vol. 7 N.S., 1855, pp. 53-89.
Vehse's "Court of Austria," vol. 7 N.S., 1855, pp. 303-335.
Dryden and his Times, vol. 7 N.S., 1855, pp. 336-367.
Evangelical Teaching — Dr. Cumming, vol. 8 N.S., 1855, pp. 436-462.
German Wit: Heinrich Heine, vol. 9 N.S., 1856, pp. 1-33.
The Natural History of German Life, vol. 10 N.S., 1856, pp. 51-79.
Silly Novels by Lady Novelists, vol. 10 N.S., 1856, pp. 442-461.
Wordliness and Other-Wordliness: the poet Young, vol. 11 N.S., 1857, pp. 1-42.
The last four, excluding "Silly Novels by Lady Novelists," were collected in a volume of "Essays" published in 1884 by Charles L. Lewes, which also includes "Leaves from a Note-Book," and from
Fraser's Magazine—
Three Months in Weimar, vol. 51, 1855, pp, 699-706.

Fortnightly Review—
The Influence of Rationalism—
Lecky's History, vol. 1, 1865,
pp. 43-55.
Blackwood's Edinburgh Magazine—
Address to Working Men, by
Felix Holt, vol. 103, 1868,
pp. 1-11.

III. SELECTIONS.

Character Readings from "George
Eliot." Selected and arranged
by N. Sheppard. New York
[1883], 8vo.
No. 293 of "Harper's Franklin
Square Library."
The George Eliot Birthday Book.
[Short extracts from the works
of George Eliot; in prose and
verse, for every day in the
year.] Edinburgh and London
[1878], 8vo.
Wise, witty, and tender sayings,
in prose and verse, selected
from the works of George Eliot
by A. Main. Edinburgh, 1872,
8vo.
——Second edition, with supple-
mentary sayings from "Middlemarch." Edinburgh, 1873, 8vo.
——Fourth edition, with supple-
mentary sayings from "Daniel
Deronda" and "Theophrastus
Such." Edinburgh and Lon-
don, 1880, 8vo.

IV. APPENDIX.

BIOGRAPHY, CRITICISM, ETC.

Acton, Lord.—George Eliot. Eine
biographische Skizze. Überset-
zung von J. Imelmann. Berlin,
1886, 8vo.
A translation of an article which
appeared in the *Nineteenth Century,*
1885.
Adams, W. H. Davenport.—Cele-
brated Englishwomen of the
Victorian Era. 2 vols. Lon-
don, 1884, 8vo.
George Eliot, vol. ii., pp. 86-182.
Ames, Charles Gordon.—George
Eliot's two marriages. An
essay. Philadelphia, 1886, 8vo.
Axon, William E. A. — Stray
Chapters in Literature, Folk-lore,
and Archæology. Manchester,
1888, 8vo.
George Eliot's Use of Dialect, pp.
161-168.
Barine, Arvède. — Portraits de
Femmes. Madame Carlyle—
George Eliot, etc. Paris, 1887,
8vo.
Blind, Mathilde.—George Eliot.
London, 1883, 8vo.
Part of the "Eminent Women
Series," edited by J. H. Ingram.
Bolton, Sarah K.—Lives of girls
who became famous. New
York [1887], 8vo.
George Eliot, pp. 213-239.
Bray, Charles.—Phases of opinion
and experience during a long
life: an autobiography. Lon-
don [1884], 8vo.
Miss M. A. Evans, pp. 72-78.
Brown, John Crombie. — The
Ethics of George Eliot's Works,
etc. Edinburgh, 1879, 8vo.
Reprinted at Philadelphia in
1885, with an introduction by C. G.
Ames, author of "George Eliot's
two marriages."
Buchanan, Robert.—A Look round
Literature. London, 1887,
8vo.
A talk with George Eliot, pp.
218-226; George Eliot's Life, pp.
314-321.

Cleveland, Rose Elizabeth. — George Eliot's Poetry and other Studies. London, 1885, 8vo.

Cone, Helen Gray, and Gilder, Jeannette L.—Pen-Portraits of Literary Women. 2 vols. New York [1888], 8vo.
George Eliot, vol. ii., pp. 245-292.

Conrad, Hermann.—George Eliot. Ihr Leben und Schaffen, etc. Berlin, 1887, 8vo.

Cooke, George Willis. — George Eliot; a critical study of her life, writings, and philosophy. London, 1883, 8vo.

Dawson, W. J.—Quest and Vision: essays in life and literature. London, 1886, 8vo.
George Eliot, pp. 158-195.

Dowden, Edward. — Studies in Literature, 1789-1877. London, 1878, 8vo.
George Eliot, pp. 240-272; "Middlemarch" and "Daniel Deronda," pp. 273-310.

Dronsart, Marie. — Portraits d'Outre-Manche. Paris, 1886, 8vo.
George Eliot, pp. 213-289.

Druskowitz, H.—Drei englische Dichterinnen Essays. Berlin, 1885, 8vo.
George Eliot, pp. 149-242.

Eliot, George.—Daniel Deronda. Versione dall' Inglese fatta con prefazione e note dell' avvocato C. Olivetti. 3 vols. Roma, 1882-83, 8vo.

——The Round Table Series, II. George Eliot, moralist and thinker. Edinburgh, 1884, 8vo.

Griswold, Hattie Tyng.—Home Life of Great Authors. Chicago, 1887, 8vo.
George Eliot, pp. 351-362.

Harrison, Frederic.—The Choice of Books, and other literary pieces. London, 1886, 8vo.
The Life of George Eliot, pp. 203-230; reprinted from the *Fortnightly Review*, March 1885.

Hazeltine, Mayo W.—Chats about Books, Poets, and Novelists. New York, 1883, 8vo.
George Eliot, pp. 1-13.

Heywood, J. C.—How they strike me, these Authors. Philadelphia, 1877, 8vo.
An Ingenious Moralist (George Eliot), pp. 57-77.

Huet, C. Busken.—Litterarische Fantasien en Kritieken. Haarlem [1883], 8vo.
George Eliot, 8th Deel, pp. 105-134.

Hutton, Richard Holt.—Essays, theological and literary. London, 1871, 8vo.
George Eliot, vol. ii., pp. 294-367.

——Essays on some of the modern guides of English thought in matters of faith. London, 1887, 8vo.
George Eliot as Author, pp. 145-258; George Eliot's Life and Letters, pp. 259-299.

James, Henry.—Partial Portraits. London, 1888, 8vo.
The Life of George Eliot, pp. 37-52; Daniel Deronda: a Conversation, pp. 65-93.

Jenkin, Fleeming.—Papers literary, scientific, etc. 2 vols. London, 1887, 8vo.
A Fragment on George Eliot, vol. i., pp. 171-174.

Kaufmann, Professor David.— George Eliot and Judaism: an attempt to appreciate " Daniel Deronda." Translated from the German. Edinburgh, 1877, 8vo.

Lancaster, Henry H.—Essays and Reviews. Edinburgh, 1876, 8vo.
George Eliot's Novels, pp. 351-398; reprinted from the *North British Review*, Sept. 1866.

Lonsdale, Margaret. — George Eliot ; thoughts upon her life, her books, and herself. London, 1886, 8vo.

McCarthy, Justin. — Modern Leaders ; being a series of Biographical Sketches. New York, 1872, 8vo.
George Eliot and George Lewes, pp. 136-144 ; appeared originally in the *Galaxy*, vol. vii., 1869, pp. 801-809.

McCrie, George.—The Religion of our Literature. Essays upon Thomas Carlyle, Robert Browning, Alfred Tennyson ; including criticisms upon the theology of George Eliot, etc. London, 1875, 8vo.

Montegut, Emile. — Ecrivains Modernes de l'Angleterre. Paris, 1885, 8vo.
George Eliot, pp. 3-180.

Morgan, William.—George Eliot : a paper read before the "Portsmouth Literary and Scientific Society," March 29th, 1881. London, 1881, 8vo.

Myers, F. W. H. — Essays, modern. London, 1883, 8vo.
George Eliot, pp. 251-275.

Parkinson, S.—Scenes from the "George Eliot" Country. With illustrations. Leeds, 1888, 8vo.

Parton, James. — Some noted Princes, Authors, and Statesmen of our time. Edited by James Parton. New York [1886] 8vo.
A meeting with George Eliot, by Mrs. John Lillie, pp. 62-65.

Paul, C. Kegan. — Biographical Sketches. London, 1883, 8vo.
George Eliot, pp. 141-170.

Robertson, Eric S. — English Poetesses : a series of critical biographies, etc. London, 1883, 8vo.
George Eliot, pp. 327-334.

Roslyn, Guy, *pseud.* [*i.e.*, Joshua Hatton]. — George Eliot in Derbyshire : a volume of gossip about passages and people in the novels of George Eliot. Reprinted from " London Society," with alterations and additions, and an introduction, by G. Barnett Smith. London, 1876, 8vo.

Russell, George W. E.—George Eliot : her genius and writings. A lecture, etc. Woburn, 1882, 8vo.

Scherer, Edmond.—Etudes Critiques sur la Littérature Contemporaine. Paris, 1863, 8vo.
George Eliot (Silas Marner), tom. i., pp. 17-27 ; reprinted from the *Temps.*

——Etudes sur la Litterature Contemporaine. Paris, 1878, 8vo.
Daniel Deronda, par George Eliot, Série v., pp. 287-304.

——Etudes sur la Littérature Contemporaine. Paris, 1885, 8vo.
George Eliot, tom. viii., pp. 187-242.

Schmidt, Julian.—Bilder aus dem Geistigen Leben unserer Zeit. 4 Bde. Leipzig, 1870-75, 8vo.
George Eliot, Bd. i., pp. 344-409.

Seguin, L. G. — Scenes and Characters from the Works of George Eliot. A series of illustrations by eminent artists, with introductory essay and descriptive letterpress by L. G. Seguin. London, 1888, 8vo.

Shepard, William.—Pen Pictures of Modern Authors. New York, 1882, 12mo.
George Eliot, pp. 41-57.

Solomon, Henry. — Daniel Deronda from a Jewish point of view. London [1877], 8vo.

Stephen, Leslie.—Article Cross, Mary Ann or Marian (*Dictionary of National Biography*, vol. xiii., pp. 216-222). London, 1888, 8vo.

Taylor, Bayard.—Critical Essays and Literary Notes. New York, 1880, 8vo.
George Eliot, pp. 339-347.

Victorian Era.—Queens of Literature of the Victorian Era. London, 1886, 8vo.
George Eliot, pp. 185-258.

Welsh, Alfred H.—Development of English Literature and Language. 2 vols. Chicago, 1882, 8vo.
George Eliot, vol. ii., pp. 470-487.

Whipple, Edwin Percy.—Recollections of Eminent Men, etc. Boston, 1887, 8vo.
Daniel Deronda, pp. 344-379; George Eliot's private life, pp. 380-397; appeared originally in the North American Review, 1885.

Wilkinson, William C.—A Free Lance in the Field of Life and Letters. New York, 1874, 8vo.
The Literary and Ethical Quality of George Eliot's Novels, pp. 1-49.

Wolzogen, Ernst von. — George Eliot. Eine biographisch-kritische Studie. Leipzig, 1885, 8vo.

MAGAZINE ARTICLES, ETC.

Eliot, George. Littell's Living Age (from the *Saturday Review*), vol. 58, 1858, pp. 274-278.—British Quarterly Review, vol. 45, 1867, pp. 141-178.—Tinsley's Magazine, vol. 3, 1868, pp. 565-

Eliot, George.

578.—Contemporary Review, by E. Dowden, vol. 20, 1872, pp. 403-422 ; same article, Eclectic Magazine, vol. 16 N.S, pp. 562-573, and Littell's Living Age, vol. 115, pp. 100-110.— St. Paul's Magazine, by Geo. B. Smith, vol. 12, 1873, pp. 592-616.—Le Correspondant, by G. de Prieux, tom. 104, 1876, pp. 672-683.—Melbourne Review, by Miss C. H. Spence, April 1876, pp. 141-163.—Victoria Magazine, vol. 31, 1878, pp. 56-60.—Nation, by W. C. Brownell, vol. 31, 1880, pp. 456, 457.— Nineteenth Century, by Edith Simcox, vol. 9, 1881, pp. 778-801; same article, Littell's Living Age, vol. 149, pp. 791-805.— Blackwood's Edinburgh Magazine, vol. 129, 1881, pp. 255-268; same article, Littell's Living Age, vol. 148, pp. 664-674, and Eclectic Magazine, vol. 33 N.S., pp. 433-443. — London Quarterly Review, vol. 57, 1881, pp. 154-176.—Cornhill Magazine, by Leslie Stephen, vol. 43, 1881, pp. 152-168; same article, Littell's Living Age, vol. 148, pp. 731-742, and Eclectic Magazine, vol. 33 N.S., pp. 443-455.—Harper's New Monthly Magazine, by C. K. Paul (illustrated), vol. 62, 1881, pp. 912-923 ; reprinted in *Biographical Sketches*, 1883. — Century Magazine, by F. W. H. Myers, vol. 23, 1881, pp. 57-64.—Literary World, by Peter Bayne, vol. 23 N.S., 1881, pp. 25, 26, 40-42, 56-58, 72-74, 89-91, 104-106, 120-122, 136-138, 152-154, 168-170, 184-186, 200-202, 216-218, 232-234, 248-250,

Eliot, George.

Matthew Browne, vol. 2, 1866, pp. 437-443.

——*and Shakespeare.* Blackwood's Edinburgh Magazine, vol. 133, 1833, pp. 524-538; same article, Eclectic Magazine, vol. 37 N.S., 1883, pp. 743-754.

——*and Thackeray, Morality of.* Atlantic Monthly, by Maria L. Henry, vol. 51, 1883, pp. 243-248.

——*and the Novel.* Critic (New York), by E. Eggleston, vol. 1, 1881, p. 9.

——*Art of.* Mind, by James Sully, vol. 6, 1881, pp. 378-394.—Fortnightly Review, by Oscar Browning, vol 43 N.S., 1888, pp. 538-553.

——*as a Christian.* Contemporary Pulpit, vol. 2, 1884, pp. 179-183.

——*as a Moral Teacher.* Westminster Review, vol. 61 N.S., 1882, pp. 65-81.

——*as a Novelist.* Westminster Review, vol. 54 N.S., 1878, pp. 105-135.

——*as a Poet.* Contemporary Review, by M. Browne, vol. 8, 1868, pp. 387-396.

——*Blind's Life of.* Athenæum, May 5, 1883, pp. 565-567.—Academy, by Eric Robertson, April 28, 1883, pp. 286, 287.—Spectator, April 28, 1883, pp. 647, 548.

——*Bray on.* Spectator, Jan. 10, 1885; same article, Critic (New York), Jan. 31, 1885, pp. 56, 57.

——*Catholic View of.* Month, vol. 42, 1881, pp. 272-278.

——*Children in Novels of.* Macmillan's Magazine, by Annie

Eliot, George.

Matheson, vol. 46, 1882, pp. 488-497; same article, Littell's Living Age, vol. 155, pp. 211-219, and Eclectic Magazine, vol. 36 N.S., 1882, pp. 822-830.

——*The Clergy as drawn by.* Charing Cross, by E. Clarke, vol. 4 N.S., 1876, pp. 295-304.

——*Cooke's Life of.* Literary World (Boston), Nov. 17, 1883, p. 381.—Academy, by Edward Dowden, Feb. 7, 1885.—Athenæum, Jan. 31 and Feb. 7, 1885.

——*Cross's Life of.* Atlantic Monthly, by Henry James, vol. 55, 1885, pp. 668-678.—Blackwood's Edinburgh Magazine, vol. 137, 1885, pp. 155-176.—British Quarterly Review, vol. 81, 1885, pp. 316-333.—Congregationalist, vol. 14, 1885, pp. 275-284. —Contemporary Review, by R. H. Hutton, vol. 47, 1885, pp. 372-391; same article, Littell's Living Age, vol. 165, pp. 3-15.—Critic (New York), Feb. 7, 1885, pp. 62, 63.—Dial (Chicago), by R. Johnson, vol. 5, 1885, pp. 289-291.—Edinburgh Review, vol. 161, 1885, pp. 514-553.—Fortnightly Review, by Frederic Harrison, vol. 37 N.S., 1885, pp. 309-322; reprinted in "The Choice of Books," etc., 1886; same article, Littell's Living Age, vol. 165, pp. 23-31.—Gentleman's Magazine, by H. R. Fox Bourne, 1885, pp. 257-271.—London Quarterly Review, vol. 64, 1885, pp. 197-222.—Macmillan's Magazine, by John Morley, vol. 51, 1885, pp. 241-256; same article, Eclectic Magazine, vol. 104, pp.

Eliot, George.

506-520, and Littell's Living
Age, vol. 164, pp 533-546.—
Nation, by A. V. Dicey, vol.
40, 1885, pp. 283, 284, 325, 326.
—New Englander, by F. H.
Stoddard, vol. 44, 1885, pp.
523-530.—Nineteenth Century,
by Lord Acton, vol. 17, 1885,
pp. 464-485.—Pall Mall Gazette,
Jan. 27 and Feb. 9, 1885.—
Pictorial World, Feb. 5 and 12,
1885.—Record, Jan. 30, 1885.
—Saturday Review, Feb. 7,
1885.—Spectator, Jan. 31, 1885.
—Time, vol. 12, 1885, pp. 374-
377.—Times, Jan. 27 and Feb.
2, 1885.—Westminster Review,
vol. 68 N.S., 1885, pp. 161-
208.

—*County of.* Century Maga
zine, by Rose G. Kingsley, vol.
30, 1885, pp. 339-352.

—*Criticisms on Contemporaries
by.* Lippincott's Magazine of
Literature, vol. 37, 1886, pp.
19-20.

—*Daniel Deronda.* Edinburgh
Review, vol. 144, 1876, pp.
442-470.—Fortnightly Review,
by Sidney Colvin, vol. 20 N.S.,
1876, pp. 601-616.—British
Quarterly Review, vol. 64,
1876, pp. 472-492 ; same article,
Eclectic Magazine, vol. 24 N.S.,
pp. 657-667. — Gentleman's
Magazine, by R. E. Francillon,
vol. 17 N.S., 1876, pp. 410-
427.—Atlantic Monthly, by
Henry James, jun., vol. 38, 1876,
pp. 684-694.—North American
Review, by E. P. Whipple, vol.
124, 1877, pp. 31-52.—Gentleman's Magazine, by J. Picciotto,
Nov. 1876, pp. 593-603.—
Victoria Magazine, by A. S.

Eliot, George.

Richardson, vol. 28, 1876, pp.
227-231. — Canadian Monthly,
vol. 9, 1876, pp. 250, 251, 343,
344 ; vol. 10, pp. 362-364.—
Nation, by A. V. Dicey, vol.
23, 1876, pp. 230, 231, 245, 246,
—Saturday Review, vol. 42,
1876, pp. 356-358.—Deutsche
Rundschau, by Wilhelm Scherer,
vol. 10, 1877, pp. 240-255.

—— ——*Deronda's Mother.* Temple Bar, vol. 49, 1877, pp. 542-
545 ; same article, Littell's
Living Age, vol. 133, pp. 248-
250, and Eclectic Magazine,
vol. 25 N.S., pp. 751-753.

—— ——*Mordecai :   a   Protest
against the Critics.* Macmillan's
Magazine, by J. Jacobs, vol. 36,
1877, pp. 101-111 ; same article,
Littell's Living Age, vol. 134,
pp. 112-121.

—*Early Life of.* Littell's
Living Age (from the *Pall Mall
Gazette*), vol. 148, 1881, pp.
381-383.

—*Essays.* Athenæum, Feb.
23, 1884, pp. 241-243 ; same
article, Littell's Living Age,
vol. 160, pp. 762-766.—Spectator, March 1, 1884. —Saturday Review, March 8, 1884.—
Academy, by H. C. Beeching,
March 15, 1884.

—*Felix Holt.* Edinburgh Review, vol. 124, 1866, pp. 435-
449 ; same article, Littell's Living Age, vol. 91, pp. 432-439.
—Blackwood's Edinburgh Magazine, vol. 100, 1866, pp. 94-109.
—Westminster Review, vol. 30
N.S., 1866, pp. 200-207.—Contemporary Review, vol. 3, 1866,
pp. 51-70.—London Quarterly
Review, vol. 27, 1866, pp. 100-

Eliot, George.

124.—North American Review, by A. G. Sedgwick, vol. 103, 1866, pp. 557-563.—Nation, by Henry James, jun., vol. 3, 1866, pp. 127, 128.—Eclectic Review, vol. 11 N.S., 1866, pp. 34-47.—Chambers's Journal, 1866, pp. 508-512.—Christian Remembrancer, vol. 52 N.S., 1866, pp. 445-468.

——*First Romance of.* Gentleman's Magazine, by R. E. Francillon, vol. 17 N.S., 1876, pp. 410-427.

——*Genius of.* Dublin Review, by William Barry, vol. 5, 3rd Series, 1881, pp. 371-394.—Southern Review, by Mrs. S. B. Herrick, vol. 13, 1873, pp. 205-235.

——*Humour of.* Spectator, Jan. 31, 1885, pp. 146, 147 ; same article, Littell's Living Age, vol. 164, pp. 638-640.

——*Ideal Ethics of.* Littell's Living Age (from the *Spectator*), vol. 142, 1879, pp. 123-125.

——*in Derbyshire.* London Society, by Guy Roslyn [Joshua Hatton], vol. 27, 1875, pp. 311-319, 439-451 ; vol. 28, pp. 20-27 ; reprinted as a separate work in 1876.

——*Last Words from.* Harper's New Monthly Magazine, by Elizabeth S. Phelps, vol. 64, 1882, pp. 568-571.

——*Later Manner of.* Canadian Monthly, vol. 11, 1878, pp. 261-268.

——*Legend of Jubal.* Macmillan's Magazine, vol. 22, 1870, pp. 1-18.

——*Life and Writings of.* International Review, by W. F. Rae,

Eliot, George.

vol. 10, pp. 447, etc., 497, etc. —Westminster Review, vol. 60 N.S., 1881, pp. 154-198.

——*Life of, illustrative of the Religious Ideas of our time.* British and Foreign Evangelical Review, by J. R. Thomson, vol. 34, 1885, pp. 517-543.

——*Literary and Ethical Quality of Novels of.* Scribner's Monthly, by W. C. Wilkinson, vol. 8, 1874, pp. 685-703.

——*Married People of.* Catholic World, by R. M. Johnston, vol. 40, 1885, pp. 620-634.

——*Middlemarch.* Quarterly Review, vol. 134, 1873, pp. 336-369.—Edinburgh Review, vol. 137, 1873, pp. 246-263.—Fortnightly Review, by Sidney Colvin, vol. 13 N.S., 1873, pp. 142-148.—Blackwood's Edinburgh Magazine, vol. 112, 1872, pp. 727-745 ; same article, Littell's Living Age, vol. 116, pp. 181-145, and Eclectic Magazine, vol. 17 N.S., pp. 215-228.—British Quarterly Review, vol. 57, 1873, pp. 407-429. — London Quarterly Review, vol. 40, 1873, pp. 99-110.—Southern Review, by Mrs. S. B. Herrick, vol. 13, 1873, pp. 205-235. — Nation, by A. V. Dicey, vol. 16, 1873, pp. 60-62, 76, 77. — North American Review, by T. S. Perry, vol. 116, 1873, pp. 432-440.—Canadian Monthly, vol. 3, 1873, pp. 549-552.—Old and New, by H. G. Spaulding, vol. 7, 1873, pp. 352-356.—Revue des Deux Mondes, by Th. Bentzon, vol. 103, 1873, pp. 667-690. —Die Gegenwart, by F. Spielhagen, Nos. 10-12, 1874.

Eliot, George.

—— ——*Middlemarch and Daniel Deronda.* Contemporary Review, by E. Dowden, vol. 29, 1877, pp. 348-369.

—— ——*Middlemarch and Fleurange, Comparison between.* Catholic World, by J. McCarthy, vol. 17, 1873, pp. 775-792.

——*Mill on the Floss.* Westminster Review, vol. 18 N.S., 1860, pp. 24-33.—Blackwood's Edinburgh Magazine, vol. 87, 1860, pp. 611 - 623. — Macmillan's Magazine, vol. 3, 1861, pp. 441-448.—Dublin University Magazine, vol. 57, 1861, pp. 192-200.

——*Moral Influence of.* Contemporary Review, vol. 39, 1881, pp. 173-185; same article, Littell's Living Age, vol. 148, pp. 561-571.

——*Morality of.* Christian World, Feb. 12, 1885.

——*Novels.* Quarterly Review, vol. 108, 1860, pp. 469-499.— National Review, vol. 11, 1860, pp. 191-219.—Christian Examiner, by I. M. Luyster, vol. 70, 1861, pp. 227-251.—Home and Foreign Review, vol. 3, 1863, pp. 522-549. — North British Review, by H. H. Lancaster, vol. 45, 1866, pp. 197-228; afterwards reprinted in "Essays and Reviews," 1876. — Macmillan's Magazine, by John Morley, vol. 14, 1866, pp. 272-279; same article, Eclectic Magazine, vol. 4 N.S., pp. 488-495.—Atlantic Monthly, by H. James, jun., vol. 18, 1866, pp. 479-492.—Scribner's Monthly, by W. C. Wilkinson, vol. 8, 1874, pp. 685-703.

Eliot, George.

——*On Mental Decay.* Knowledge, by R. A. Proctor, Aug. 14, 1885, pp. 127-129.

——*On the Gospel.* Christian World, Feb. 28, 1884.

——*Opinions about Religion.* Month, vol. 53, 1885, pp. 473-482.

——*Poems.* North American Review, by H. James, jun., vol. 119, 1874, pp. 484-489.

——*Politics of.* Gentleman's Magazine, by F. Dolman, vol. 259, 1885, pp. 294-300; same article, Eclectic Magazine, vol. 42 N.S., pp. 675-679.

——*Portrait of.* Century Magazine, vol. 23, 1881, pp. 47, 48.

——*Private Life of.* North American Review, by E. P. Whipple, vol. 141, 1885, p. 320, etc. ; afterwards reprinted in *Recollections of Eminent Men,* 1887.

——*Religion of.* Dublin Review, by William Barry, vol 6, Third Series, 1881, pp. 433-464.— Christian World, January 29, 1885.

——*Reminiscences of.* Graphic, Jan. 8, 1881.

——*Romola.* Westminster Review, vol. 24 N.S., 1863, pp. 344-351. — Blackwood's Edinburgh Magazine, vol. 116, 1874, pp. 72-91.—Christian Remembrancer, vol. 52 N.S., 1866, pp. 468-479.—Revue des Deux Mondes, by E. D. Forgues, vol. 48, 1863, pp. 939-967.

—— ——*In Florence with Romola.* Scribner's Magazine (illustrated), by E. H. and E. W.

Eliot, George.
Blashfield, vol. 2, 1887, pp.
693-721.

——*Rustic of, and Thomas Hardy.*
Merry England, by C. Kegan
Paul, vol. 1, 1883, pp. 40-51.

—— *Scenes of Clerical Life.*
Saturday Review, vol. 5, 1858,
pp. 566, 567.

——*Silas Marner.* Revue des
Deux Mondes, by Cucheval-
Clarigny, tom. 35, 1861, pp.
188-210.

—— —— *Silas Marner and
Holmes's Elsie Venner.* Macmillan's Magazine, vol. 4, 1861,
pp. 305-309.

——*Sonnet on.* Temple Bar, vol.
67, 1883, p. 123, and also in
the Eclectic Magazine, vol. 38
N.S., p. 80.

——*Spanish Gypsy.* Edinburgh
Review, vol. 128, 1868, pp.
523-538.—Westminster Review,
vol. 34 N.S., 1868, pp. 183-192.
—London Quarterly Review,
vol. 31, 1868, pp. 160-188.—
Blackwood's Edinburgh Magazine, vol. 103, 1868, pp. 760-
771.—British Quarterly Review,
vol. 48, 1868, pp. 503-534.—
Fraser's Magazine, by J. Skelton,
vol. 78, 1868, pp. 468-479.—
Macmillan's Magazine, by John
Morley, vol. 18, 1868, pp. 281-
287; same article, Eclectic
Magazine, vol. 8 N.S., pp. 1276-
1282.—St. James's Magazine,
vol. 1 N.S., 1868, pp. 478-486.
—St. Paul's, vol. 2, 1868, pp.
583-592.—North American Review, by Henry James, jun.,
vol. 107, 1868, pp. 620-635.—
Nation, vol. 7, 1868, pp. 12-14.
—Revue des Deux Mondes, by

Eliot, George.
Louis Etienne, tom. 90, 1870,
pp. 429-446.

——*Surrender of Faith by.*
British and Foreign Evangelical Review, by W. G. Blackie,
vol. 35, 1886, pp. 38-65.

——*Theophrastus Such.* Edin-
burgh Review, vol. 150, 1879,
pp. 557-586.—Fortnightly Re-
view, by Grant Allen, vol. 26
N.S., 1879, pp. 145-149.—
Westminster Review, vol. 56
N.S., 1879, pp. 185-196.—
Fraser's Magazine, vol. 20
N.S., 1879, pp. 103-124.—
Canadian Monthly, vol. 3, 1879,
pp. 333-335.—British Quarterly
Review, vol. 70, 1879, pp. 240-
242.—North American Review,
vol. 129, 1879, pp. 510-513.

——*Village Life according to*
Fraser's Magazine, by T. E.
Kebbel, vol. 23 N.S., 1881, pp.
263-276; same article, Littell's
Living Age, vol. 148, pp. 608-
617.

——*A Week with.* Temple Bar,
vol. 73, 1885, pp. 226-232;
same article, Critic (New York),
March 7, 1885, pp. 116,117, and
Littell's Living Age, vol. 164,
pp. 743-746.

—— *Work of.* Le Correspondant,
by Pierre du Quesnoy, tom. 113,
1878, pp. 438-470, 660-682, 826-
847.

——*Works of.* British Quarterly
Review, vol. 45, 1867, pp. 141-
178.—Revue des Deux Mondes,
by Arvède Barine, tom. 70,
1885, pp. 100-130.—Revue des
Deux Mondes, by Emile Montegut, tom. 56, 1883, pp. 305-346.

V. CHRONOLOGICAL LIST OF WORKS.

Strauss's Life of Jesus (*Trans.*) . . . 1846	Legend of Jubal and other poems 1874
Feuerbach's Essence of Christianity (*Trans.*) . 1854	Daniel Deronda . . 1876
Scenes of Clerical Life . 1858	Impressions of Theophrastus Such 1879
Adam Bede . . . 1859	
The Mill on the Floss . 1860	
Silas Marner . . . 1861	
Romola 1863	
Felix Holt . . . 1866	Essays and Leaves from a Note-Book . . . 1884
The Spanish Gypsy . . 1868	
Agatha 1869	Life, as related in her letters
Middlemarch . . 1871, 72	and journals . . . 1885

Printed by WALTER SCOTT, *Felling, Newcastle-on-Tyne.*

For EU product safety concerns, contact us at Calle de José Abascal, 56–1°,
28003 Madrid, Spain or eugpsr@cambridge.org.

www.ingramcontent.com/pod-product-compliance
Ingram Content Group UK Ltd.
Pitfield, Milton Keynes, MK11 3LW, UK
UKHW012344130625
459647UK00009B/510